Learning from jQuery

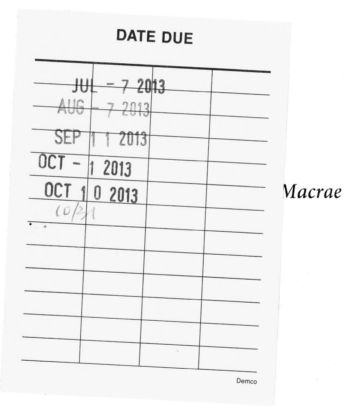
Macrae

O'REILLY®

Beijing · Cambridge · Farnham · Köln · Sebastopol · Tokyo

Learning from jQuery

by Callum Macrae

Copyright © 2013 Callum Macrae. All rights reserved.

Printed in the United States of America.

Published by O'Reilly Media, Inc., 1005 Gravenstein Highway North, Sebastopol, CA 95472.

O'Reilly books may be purchased for educational, business, or sales promotional use. Online editions are also available for most titles (*http://my.safaribooksonline.com*). For more information, contact our corporate/institutional sales department: 800-998-9938 or *corporate@oreilly.com*.

Editors: Simon St.Laurent and Meghan Blanchette
Production Editor: Rachel Steely

Copyeditor: Rachel Monaghan
Proofreader: Kiel Van Horn
Cover Designer: Randy Corner
Interior Designer: David Futato
Illustrator: Rebecca Demarest

February 2013:   First Edition.

Revision History for the First Edition.:

2013-01-28   First release

See *http://oreilly.com/catalog/errata.csp?isbn=9781449335199* for release details.

ISBN: 978-1-449-33519-9

[LSI]

Table of Contents

Preface

Many developers are comfortable with using the jQuery library, which adds features to JavaScript and makes a lot of tasks easier, but they are slightly less confident when using JavaScript without jQuery. This could be because they don't like the syntax of JavaScript and so try to avoid writing pure JavaScript as much as possible, or it could just be because they're hoping that they'll never have to work on a project where they can't use jQuery. Whatever the reason, this can result in the parts of their code that aren't using jQuery being inefficient or incorrect.

If any of this sounds like you, then this book provides an opportunity for you to expand your knowledge of the bits of JavaScript that jQuery covers up for you. In the first four chapters, we'll cover event handling, prototypes, working with the DOM, and AJAX. Chapter 5 is about conventions in JavaScript, and covers some common conventions and patterns in JavaScript. There are also two appendixes: Appendix A aims to teach JavaScript to someone who has never written it without jQuery before, and Appendix B highlights some useful tools that you can use to aid you when coding.

You can find all the major functions from this book, such as the AJAX and event functions, and some additional code samples, on this GitHub repo (*http://bit.ly/ V3P0ia*).

Who This Book Is For

This book is targeted at developers who know jQuery, but who don't yet feel confident in their JavaScript knowledge or would just like to know more. You don't need to know everything there is to know about jQuery, as I'll be explaining what something does if it isn't already obvious—for example, I wouldn't explain what `.fadeIn()` does, as it is descriptive enough that it doesn't require explanation.

Who This Book Isn't For

This book assumes a basic knowledge of jQuery, and I wouldn't recommend reading it if you have no experience in JavaScript or jQuery. If that describes you, I would recommend finding a basic JavaScript book such as Michael Morrison's *Head First JavaScript* (*http://oreil.ly/HF_JavaScript*), David Sawyer McFarland's *JavaScript and jQuery: The Missing Manual* (*http://oreil.ly/JavaScript_jQuery_TMM*), or Shelley Powers's *Learning JavaScript* (*http://oreil.ly/Learning_JavaScript*). For a more comprehensive exploration, try David Flanagan's *JavaScript: The Definitive Guide* (*http://oreil.ly/ JS_Definitive_Guide*).

While it certainly won't hurt, this book wasn't written for you if you already consider yourself fairly good with JavaScript, and you may not learn much. You won't have covered everything in the book (especially in Chapter 5), but a lot of it will likely be material you already know.

Conventions Used in This Book

The following typographical conventions are used in this book:

Italic

Indicates new terms, URLs, email addresses, filenames, and file extensions.

`Constant width`

Used for program listings, as well as within paragraphs to refer to program elements such as variable or function names, databases, data types, environment variables, statements, and keywords.

`Constant width bold`

Shows commands or other text that should be typed literally by the user.

`Constant width italic`

Shows text that should be replaced with user-supplied values or by values determined by context.

This icon signifies a tip, suggestion, or general note.

This icon indicates a warning or caution.

Using Code Examples

This book is here to help you get your job done. In general, if this book includes code examples, you may use the code in this book in your programs and documentation. You do not need to contact us for permission unless you're reproducing a significant portion of the code. For example, writing a program that uses several chunks of code from this book does not require permission. Selling or distributing a CD-ROM of examples from O'Reilly books does require permission. Answering a question by citing this book and quoting example code does not require permission. Incorporating a significant amount of example code from this book into your product's documentation does require permission.

We appreciate, but do not require, attribution. An attribution usually includes the title, author, publisher, and ISBN. For example: "*Learning from jQuery* by Callum Macrae (O'Reilly). Copyright 2013 Callum Macrae, 978-1-449-33519-9."

If you feel your use of code examples falls outside fair use or the permission given above, feel free to contact us at *permissions@oreilly.com*.

Safari® Books Online

Safari Books Online is an on-demand digital library that delivers expert content in both book and video form from the world's leading authors in technology and business.

Technology professionals, software developers, web designers, and business and creative professionals use Safari Books Online as their primary resource for research, problem solving, learning, and certification training.

Safari Books Online offers a range of product mixes and pricing programs for organizations, government agencies, and individuals. Subscribers have access to thousands of books, training videos, and prepublication manuscripts in one fully searchable database from publishers like O'Reilly Media, Prentice Hall Professional, Addison-Wesley Professional, Microsoft Press, Sams, Que, Peachpit Press, Focal Press, Cisco Press, John Wiley & Sons, Syngress, Morgan Kaufmann, IBM Redbooks, Packt, Adobe Press, FT Press, Apress, Manning, New Riders, McGraw-Hill, Jones & Bartlett, Course Technology, and dozens more. For more information about Safari Books Online, please visit us online.

How to Contact Us

Please address comments and questions concerning this book to the publisher:

> O'Reilly Media, Inc.
> 1005 Gravenstein Highway North
> Sebastopol, CA 95472
> 800-998-9938 (in the United States or Canada)
> 707-829-0515 (international or local)
> 707-829-0104 (fax)

We have a web page for this book, where we list errata, examples, and any additional information. You can access this page at: *http://oreil.ly/Learning_jQuery*

To comment or ask technical questions about this book, send email to *bookques tions@oreilly.com*.

For more information about our books, courses, conferences, and news, see our website at *http://www.oreilly.com*.

Find us on Facebook: *http://facebook.com/oreilly*

Follow us on Twitter: *http://twitter.com/oreillymedia*

Watch us on YouTube: *http://www.youtube.com/oreillymedia*

Acknowledgments

Thank you to David DeMello, Eric Hamilton, Cody Lindley, and Ralph Whitbeck, the technical reviewers without whom this book wouldn't be half what it is now. Thanks also to my editors, Meghan Blanchette and Simon St.Laurent, and everyone else at O'Reilly Media.

A massive thanks to all the folks at webdevRefinery for motivating me to write this book in the first place.

Finally, I'd like to thank John Resig and everyone else who has contributed to the wonderful jQuery library. Without jQuery, I would be stuck spending half my time debugging Internet Explorer issues!

CHAPTER 1

Event Handling

In JavaScript, an *event* is the result of an action that can be detected by JavaScript—for example, the user clicking a button or the page load completing. Events are the heart of pretty much all web applications. Event handling, as you can probably tell by the name, is how we handle these events.

jQuery provides a suite of functions to make event handling considerably easier than in JavaScript alone. While this is nice, it can add overhead and remove control from you, the developer. For this reason, it is important to know how you can handle events without jQuery in pure JavaScript. In this chapter, I'll be covering that as well as a few other topics that can help your jQuery knowledge, such as more about what events actually are and how they work.

Internet Explorer 8 and below does event handling completely differently than any other browser, and completely independently from any standards. If you're writing an application that needs to support 99% of the market share and you cannot use jQuery, then you will need to write for these older browsers—even IE6 still has an over 5% market share at the time of writing. This chapter will cover event handling in Internet Explorer as well as in other browsers.

Listening for Events

Events in jQuery

The best way to explain events is probably by using an example, and the best example (as I'm assuming that you know jQuery) is to show an extract of jQuery code that works with events. The following code turns the anchor element with ID `foo` red when it is clicked, and then prevents the link from being followed by calling `e.preventDe fault()`:

```
$('a#foo').click(function (e) {
        $(this).css('color', 'red');
        e.preventDefault();
});
```

Events in JavaScript

Following is the same code, but in pure JavaScript. It will not work in IE8 and below, which we will cover in the next section:

```
var foo = document.getElementById('foo');
foo.addEventListener('click', function (e) {
        this.style.color = 'red';
        e.preventDefault();
});
```

The .addEventListener function accepts three arguments. The first is the event type, and the second is the callback to be called when the event is fired. The third argument allows you to specify whether the event should be capturing or bubbling (i.e., the order in which it should propagate in; I'll explain this later), but as IE8 and below don't support that, it isn't commonly used. The callback is sent the event as an argument, which contains a lot of information—such as the *x* and *y* positions of the mouse when it clicked the element, and information on elements such as the current element and the element from which the event was fired (they can be different if the event has propagated). It also has some useful methods such as .preventDefault() and .stop Propagation(). The callback is called with the element as the context, so the element can be referred to using this. Unlike with jQuery, the return value doesn't do anything at all.

.preventDefault() stops the default action from happening. For example, if we had a link to some website with ID foo (<a href="http://example.com" id="foo">Click here!</a>) and we ran the previous code, clicking the link would not go to that website, as the call to e.preventDefault() would prevent it (following the link is the default action).

In jQuery, you can also return false to prevent the default action. However, this also stops the event from propagating (we will cover event propagation later), which is generally undesired.

Events in Internet Explorer 8

Internet Explorer 9 introduced support for .addEventListener, and so can use the preceding code. However, earlier IE versions don't support it, so we have to use another function, .attachEvent. It only supports bubbling events, and you can't refer to the element using `this`; you have to use either `e.target` or `e.srcElement` (although it is easier to just save the element from earlier). It also doesn't support `e.preventDe fault()`; we have to set `e.returnValue` to `false` instead. Following is the same code from the previous two examples, but for Internet Explorer 8:

```
var foo = document.getElementById('foo');
foo.attachEvent('onclick', function (e) {

        // Either:
        foo.style.color = 'red';

        // Or:
        ((e.target) ? e.target : e.srcElement).style.color = 'red';

        e.returnValue = false;
});
```

Writing a Wrapper Function

jQuery makes it very easy to bind events to objects in every browser, but it isn't always necessary to load the entire jQuery library just to use the event handling functions, which can be replicated fairly easily. I'll give you some code, and then I will explain how it works:

```
function addEventListener(element, event, handler) {
        if (element.addEventListener) {
                element.addEventListener(event, handler);
        } else if (element.attachEvent) {
                element.attachEvent('on' + event, function (e) {
                        e.preventDefault = function () {
                                e.returnValue = false;
                        };

                        handler.call(element, e);
                });
        }
}
```

We can then call it using the following code (in any browser):

```
var foo = document.getElementById('foo');
addEventListener(foo, 'click', function (e) {
        this.style.color = 'red';
        e.preventDefault();
});
```

The `addEventListener` function first checks whether the element has the `.addEvent Listener` method, and if so, then it calls it normally. If it doesn't exist, the function checks whether the `.attachEvent` method exists, and if so, then it calls `function` as the handler. When the anonymous function is called, it calls the actual handler using `.call`, which allows us to specify the scope to be used as the first argument, meaning that we can refer to the element using `this`.

To enable us to use the `e.preventDefault()` function in Internet Explorer, I'm adding that function to the event, and when it is called, I'm setting `e.returnValue` to `false`. We could also do this the other way around using the following, but I won't be keeping this code as we develop this function throughout the chapter because it isn't standard-conforming like `e.preventDefault()`:

```
function addEventListener(element, event, handler) {
    if (element.addEventListener) {
        element.addEventListener(event, function (e) {
            handler.call(this, e);

            if (e.returnValue === false) {
                e.preventDefault();
            }
        });
    } else if (element.attachEvent) {
        element.attachEvent('on' + event, function (e) {
            handler.call(element, e);
        });
    }
}
```

That can be called as follows in any browser:

```
var foo = document.getElementById('foo');
addEventListener(foo, 'click', function (e) {
    this.style.color = 'red';
    e.returnValue = false;
});
```

We can also replicate jQuery's `return false` behavior by checking the return value of the event handler:

```
function addEventListener(element, event, handler) {
    if (element.addEventListener) {
        element.addEventListener(event, function (e) {
            if (handler.call(this, e) === false) {
                e.preventDefault();
            }
        });
    } else if (element.attachEvent) {
        element.attachEvent('on' + event, function (e) {
            if (handler.call(element, e) === false) {
                e.returnValue = false;
```

```
                }
            });
        }
    }
```

That can be called as follows in any browser:

```
var foo = document.getElementById('foo');
addEventListener(foo, 'click', function (e) {
        this.style.color = 'red';
        return false;
});
```

A lot of websites and web-based applications have completely dropped support for Internet Explorer versions earlier than 9, so they do not need to use a wrapper function or `.attachEvent`, and can just use `.addEventListener`. This reduces development and testing time, and therefore costs less—but it does remove support for a substantial chunk of the browser market.

I'm not going to cover this in any more detail than a brief mention here, but before DOM 3 was specified, events were attached to elements inline. You may have seen something like the following code before:

```
<a href="#" onclick="this.style.color = 'red'">Click to turn red!</a>
```

That code is pretty ugly, right? Not only is it very tricky to read, it is also very difficult to maintain. Inline JavaScript and CSS is now frowned upon for those reasons, and JavaScript and CSS should always be kept in external files. It isn't commonly used anymore, so I won't be mentioning it again.

Adding Event Handlers to Multiple Elements

Sometimes it may be useful to add event listeners to multiple elements. There are two different ways to do this: either we can cycle through the elements and add the event handler to each one, or we can add the event handler to a common parent of the elements, and wait for it to bubble up—see the section "Event Propagation" (page 7). The second method is generally preferred because it uses fewer resources, but if there are only a few elements, it can be overkill. The first method is more commonly used.

jQuery does both methods automatically. We can do the first method like this:

```
$('.bar').click(callback);
```

And the second like this:

```
$(document).on('click', '.bar', callback);
```

JavaScript does not do this automatically. Attempting to call .addEventListener or .attachEvent on a list of elements will throw an error because it isn't defined, and calling the previously defined addEventListener function just won't do anything, as it won't be able to find either method. In order to attach an event to multiple elements, we have to loop through them:

```
var bars = document.getElementsByClassName('bar');
for (var i = 0; i < bars.length; i++) {
        addEventListener(bars[i], 'click', callback);
}
```

document.getElementsByClassName returns a NodeList, not an array. One main difference between the two is that NodeLists update live, meaning that changes to the DOM also change the NodeList:

```
var paragraphs = document.getElementsByTagName('p');
console.log(paragraphs.length); // 3

// Create a new paragraph element and append it to the body

console.log(paragraphs.length); // 4
```

Occasionally, this can result in an infinite loop in the page: say you have a function that loops through all paragraph elements, and then copies them to the end of a page. This will also copy them to the end of the NodeList, meaning that they will also be copied to the end of the page again, and again, and again...

There are two ways to avoid this. The first is to cache the length of the NodeList:

```
var paragraphs = document.getElementsByTagName('p');
for (var i = 0, len = paragraphs.length; i < len; i++) {
        document.body.appendChild(paragraphs[i].clone(true));
}
```

This means that if the original length of the NodeList were three, then it would only clone three elements before stopping. The second approach would be to turn the NodeList into an array:

```
var paragraphs = document.getElementsByTagName('p');
paragraphs = Array.prototype.slice.call(paragraphs);
for (var i = 0; i < paragraphs.length; i++) {
        document.body.appendChild(paragraphs[i].clone(true));
}
```

We did this by calling the Array.slice method directly on the NodeList, causing it to treat it like an array. We can call other array methods on the NodeList using the same method; in the following example, we loop through all elements with a data-number attribute and return an array containing all of them:

```
var elements = document.querySelectorAll('[data-number]');
var numbers = Array.prototype.map.call(elements, function (element) {
```

```
        return Number(element.dataset.number); // Get the data-number attribute
    });

    console.log(numbers); // [3, 6, 2, 5.6]
```

Of course, it is easier to just use jQuery:

```
    var numbers = $('[data-number]').map(function () {
        return $(this).data('number');
    });

    console.log(numbers); // [3, 6, 2, 5.6]
```

jQuery's `$.fn.data` function automatically converts number strings to actual numbers. If you don't want this behavior, you should use `$.fn.attr`.

Event Propagation

When an event is fired on an element, it isn't just fired for the specific element, it is also fired for all parent elements of that element. This can be pretty useful for setting an event listener on multiple elements at the same time without having to loop through them one by one:

```
    document.addEventListener('click', function (e) {
        var element = e.srcElement;
        if (element.tagName === 'A') {
            var url = getAnchorURL(element);
            if (isEvil(url)) {
                e.preventDefault();

                // Inform user that they clicked an "evil" link
            }
        }
    });
```

That code would add a listener for all clicks on anything in the document. When an element with `tagName` "A" (an anchor element) is clicked, it checks whether the URL is "evil" (e.g., linking to a dangerous site), and if so, it calls `e.preventDefault()`, preventing the user from following the link. We have to use `e.srcElement` instead of `this`, as `this` would refer to the document because that is what the event is being fired on.

jQuery's `.on` method has this behavior built in. There is an optional second parameter that allows you to specify a selector. If the selector matches the source element (`e.srcElement`), then the event listener is fired. In effect, the following code does the same thing as the previous:

```
    $(document).on('click', 'a', function () {
        var element = e.srcElement,
            url = getAnchorURL(element);
```

```
        if (isEvil(url)) {
                e.preventDefault();

                // Inform user that they clicked an "evil" link
        }
});
```

The action of events being fired on the parent elements is called *event propagation*. The order in which they are fired is called the *event order*. There are two possible event orders that they can be fired in: bubbling and capturing.

When an event *bubbles*, it is fired first on the element itself, and then all of its parents respectively; see Figure 1-1 for a graphical visualization. I find this event order to generally be the most useful.

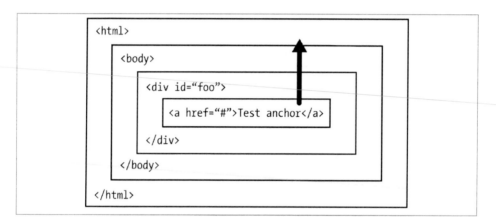

Figure 1-1. A bubbling event

When an event "captures," it is fired first on the document body, and then works its way down the tree to the element itself—see Figure 1-2.

Both methods can be useful. addEventListener has a third parameter that allows you to specify the order in which you want the event to propagate: true or unspecified for bubbling, or false for capturing. attachEvent doesn't support capturing event listeners at all, and so Internet Explorer 8 and below only supports bubbling events.

Going back to our original code sample to stop evil links from being clicked, we can see that it should probably be a capturing event listener rather than a bubbling event listener, as capturing event listeners are called first (see Figure 1-3). This means that if we call e.stopPropagation(), any event listeners added to the element itself won't be called, so the link has a lower chance of being followed. Our new code, using capturing event propagation, is as follows:

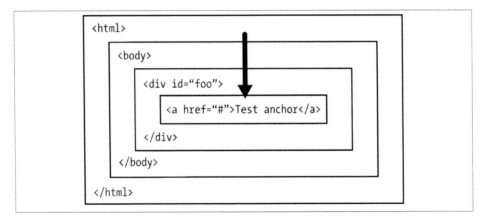

Figure 1-2. A capturing event

```
document.addEventListener('click', function (e) {
        var element = e.srcElement;
        if (element.tagName === 'A') {
                var url = getAnchorURL(element);
                if (isEvil(url)) {
                        e.preventDefault();
                        e.stopPropagation();

                        // Inform user that they clicked an "evil" link
                }
        }
}, false);
```

So which are fired first, bubbling or captured event listeners? Does the event start at the element, bubble up, and then capture back down again, or does it start at the document? The WC3 specifies that events should capture down from the document, and then bubble back up again, which you can see in Figure 1-3.

So, say we have the following document:

```
<!DOCTYPE html>
<html>
<body>
        <div id="foo">
                <a href="#">Test anchor</a>
        </div>
</body>
</html>
```

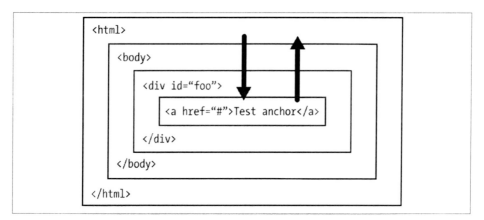

Figure 1-3. Capturing and then bubbling

If we click on the anchor, the events will be fired in the following order:

1. On the document (capturing)
2. On the body (capturing)
3. On div#foo (capturing)
4. On the anchor (capturing)
5. On the anchor (bubbling)
6. On div#foo (bubbling)
7. On the body (bubbling)
8. On the document (bubbling)

Internet Explorer's .attachEvent

.attachEvent has a couple more problems besides not supporting capturing events. With .addEventListener, the listener is called with this referring to the element on which the listener was fired (for example, the document or the body, not necessarily the anchor). The event also has a .currentTarget property containing the element. With .attachEvent, this refers to the window object and .currentTarget is undefined with no equivalent property, so if the same event listener is assigned to multiple elements we have no way of determining which element the event is being fired.

It also doesn't have the `e.stopPropagation()` method, and instead has a `.cancelBub`ble property that must be set to `true` to cancel propagation. The equivalent of the code sample that I have been using throughout this section would be:

```
var elements = document.getElementsByTagName('a');
for (var i = 0; i < elements.length; i++) {
        (function (element) {
                element.attachEvent('onclick', function (e) {
                        var url = getAnchorURL(element);
                        if (isEvil(url)) {
                                e.returnValue = false;
                                e.cancelBubble = true;

                                // Inform user that they clicked an "evil" link
                        }
                });
        })(elements[i]);
}
```

We'll add a fake `e.stopPropagation` method to our `addEventListener` function so that we can use it in our event listeners without having to test whether it exists:

```
function addEventListener(element, event, handler) {
        if (element.addEventListener) {
                element.addEventListener(event, handler);
        } else if (element.attachEvent) {
                element.attachEvent('on' + event, function (e) {
                        e.preventDefault = function () {
                                e.returnValue = false;
                        };
                        e.stopPropagation = function () {
                                e.cancelBubble = true;
                        };

                        handler.call(element, e);
                });
        }
}
```

Triggering Events

To trigger an event in jQuery, we can simply use the `.trigger` method on the element, which will simulate the event being triggered. It doesn't, however, actually trigger a JavaScript event—it just cycles through all events set by `.on` (or any of the aliases, such as `.click`) and calls them. This means that it will only trigger event handlers set by jQuery, and any event handlers set using `addEventListener` will be ignored. There is no way to trigger events set using JavaScript using only jQuery.

To trigger events the way jQuery does it, we would have to have an array of events to which addEventListener adds whenever it is called, and then when .trigger is called, we'd have to cycle through them, executing the events that match the event type and element. Then, it would get slightly more complicated, as we would have to go up the tree, calling the event listeners for each parent element until something stops propagation or we hit the <html> element. This isn't that difficult, though, as every element has a .parentElement property that returns an element's parent. It'll only return the one element, so we don't need to worry about cycling through them, as it will not return a NodeList.

We're going to focus on the other method of triggering events, as we want it to work with event handlers added with pure JavaScript. It's a lot trickier than the way jQuery does it—again, IE does it differently—but it is the only way that works when event listeners have been added via the standard JavaScript APIs (.addEventListener).

First, we create the event using document.createEvent, and then we dispatch it using the dispatchEvent method on the element. Sounds simple, right? It isn't. I'll give you a generic solution, but there are many different types of events, and for each to work correctly, the methods called and arguments given to them need to be slightly different. Here is the generic solution:

```
var element = document.getElementById('foo');
var event = document.createEvent('UIEvents');
event.initUIEvent('click', true, true, window, 1);
var returned = element.dispatchEvent(event);
```

returned is set to the return value of any event handlers triggered. This can be useful for replicating jQuery's functionality where the developer can return false to prevent the default action:

```
var element = document.getElementById('foo');

element.addEventListener('click', function () {
        return false;
});

var element = document.getElementById('foo');
var event = document.createEvent('UIEvents');
event.initUIEvent('click', true, true, window, 1);
var returned = element.dispatchEvent(event);

if (returned === false) {
        event.preventDefault();
}
```

That code should successfully call any event handlers, but it doesn't set any of the often useful properties like the x and y positions of the mouse; if you want them, you will have to set them by modifying the event object:

```
var event = document.createEvent('UIEvents');
event.initUIEvent('click', true, true, window, 1);

event.x = 100;
event.y = 50;

var returned = element.dispatchEvent(event);
```

The event automatically bubbles, so there is no need to simulate that like you would have to with the other method.

Triggering Events in Internet Explorer 8

Syntax-wise, triggering events in Internet Explorer is fairly similar to triggering events in other browsers, but it uses different functions. The following code fires the click event on the element with ID foo:

```
var element = document.getElementById('foo');
element.fireEvent('onclick');
```

element.fireEvent has an optional second parameter: the event. It can be used like so:

```
var element = document.getElementById('foo');
var event = document.createEventObject();
event.button = 1;
element.fireEvent('onclick', event);
```

Again, if you want properties like the *x* and *y* positions of the mouse, you'll have to add them yourself. event.button = 1 tells the event that it is a left click.

It's a lot less generic, and you can't usually just change the name of the function without weird side effects—you would have to customize the code more for behavior like mouseover events.

Writing a Wrapper Function to Trigger Events

Writing a wrapper function for triggering events without a massive switch statement is difficult, and a tad hacky. I would usually recommend either having a function for each type of event you want to fire, or doing it how jQuery does it and storing an object of events that have been set. I've written the following wrapper function, but I wouldn't really recommend using it; it is just to show you how you can use a single function to fire events in all browsers:

```
function triggerEvent(element, event) {
        if (element.dispatchEvent) {
                var evt = document.createEvent('UIEvents');
                evt.initUIEvent(event, true, true, window, 1);
                element.dispatchEvent(evt);
        } else if (element.fireEvent) {
```

```
        // Internet Explorer support
        var evt = document.createEventObject();
        evt.button = 1;
        element.fireEvent('on' + event, evt);
    } else if (element['on' + event]) {
        element['on' + event].call();
    }
}
```

The last statement is to demonstrate how this function can work for older browsers that still use DOM 2. If the event has been initiated via the onclick attribute and the browser doesn't support either .dispatchEvent or .fireEvent, then you can manually run the code using .call().

 To trigger events on multiple elements, you can use the same method that we used to add event handlers to multiple elements: loop through them.

Removing Event Handlers

To remove an event in jQuery, we can just use the .off method on the element:

```
function clickHandler(){}
$('#foo').click(clickHandler);

// Either:
$('#foo').off('click', clickHandler);

// Or:
$('#foo').off('click');
```

The difference between the two calls to .off is that the first removes only the handler specified as the second argument, while the second removes all click handlers. Calling .off with no arguments would remove all event handlers of every type from that element (at least, ones set with jQuery). Note that you have to pass the exact function that you set, or the handler won't be removed. The following code, for example, will not remove the event handler:

```
// Does not work:
$('#foo').click(function (){});
$('#foo').off('click', function (){});
```

To remove an event handler in JavaScript, use JavaScript's .removeEventListener method. It doesn't work in Internet Explorer 8:

```
var foo = document.getElementById('foo');
function clickHandler(){}

addEventListener(foo, 'click', clickHandler);
foo.removeEventListener('click', clickHandler);
```

If we neglect to provide the last argument to .removeEventListener, then an error will be thrown. If you want to remove all event listeners of a certain event, you have to keep a record of them as you add them, and loop through them, removing them one by one (wrapper functions are very useful for this).

Removing Event Handlers in Internet Explorer 8

To remove event handlers in Internet Explorer, we have to use the .detachEvent function. It's fairly similar to .removeEventHandler:

```
var foo = document.getElementById('foo');
function clickHandler(){}

addEventListener(foo, 'click', clickHandler);
foo.detachEvent('onclick', clickHandler);
```

Writing a Wrapper Function to Remove Events

As shown previously with triggering events, here I have written another basic wrapper function—but in this case, to remove events in all browsers:

```
function removeEventListener(element, event, handler) {
        if (element.removeEventListener) {
                element.removeEventListener(event, handler);
        } else if (element.detachEvent) {
                element.detachEvent('on' + event, handler);
        }
}
```

Unfortunately, this won't be able to remove events set via addEventListener in Internet Explorer, as that function gives element.attachEvent a different callback than the one given to addEventListener. We can work around this by modifying addEventListener to store the old callbacks and new callbacks in an object or array, which we can then loop through in removeEventListener to find the new callback.

As noted, we could use either an object or array: in an object, we would somehow turn the original function into the key (if we just use the function as the key, then functions with the same code will override each other because they will be converted to strings) and store the functions by those keys. Then when we go to remove the event listener, we will turn the function back into the key using the same method, and then the generated callback will be grabbed and removed. To use an array, we would simply push the original function and the new function to an array and cycle through the array to find the event listener when we go to remove it. For the sake of simplicity, I'll use an array in the following examples.

Our new addEventListener:

```
var listeners = [];
function addEventListener(element, event, handler) {
        if (element.addEventListener) {
                element.addEventListener(event, handler);
        } else if (element.attachEvent) {
                var newHandler = function (e) {
                        e.preventDefault = function () {
                                e.returnValue = false;
                        };
                        e.stopPropagation = function () {
                                e.cancelBubble = true;
                        };

                        handler.call(element, e);
                };
                element.attachEvent('on' + event, newHandler);
                listeners.push([handler, newHandler]);
        }
}
```

And the updated removeEventListener with support for Internet Explorer 8 and below:

```
function removeEventListener(element, event, handler) {
    if (element.removeEventListener) {
                element.removeEventListener(event, handler);
        } else if (element.detachEvent) {
                event = 'on' + event;
                for (var i = 0; i < listeners.length; i++) {
                        if (listeners[i][0] === handler) {
                                element.detachEvent(event, listeners[i][1]);
                                break;
                        }
                }
        }
}
```

Adding a "Once Only" Event Listener

jQuery's .one method adds an event listener that will only be called once; once we call the event listener the first time, it will be removed and thus will not be called again. To do this in pure JavaScript, store a copy of the function in an object and then, in the event handler itself, call removeEventListener.

Summary

This chapter has shown how you can use `.addEventListener` (and `.attachEvent` in Internet Explorer 8 and below) to add event handlers, and how you can use `removeEventListener` (and `detachEvent` in Internet Explorer 8 and below) to remove them. It has explained the basic concepts of triggering events, as well as how events propagate.

CHAPTER 2

Constructors and Prototypes

Constructors are a way of creating objects, and can be initiated via the new keyword. Many instances of an object can be created. Prototypes are one of the more powerful features of JavaScript, and allow the developer to declare a method or property that all instances of an object will inherit.

This chapter is less about building on your existing jQuery knowledge than teaching you a method you can use to enhance your jQuery code. To an extent, it will also help you understand how jQuery works, as jQuery itself uses prototypes.

Constructors

Constructors are functions that are called by the new keyword. For example:

```
function Greeting(item) {
        this.log = function () {
                console.log('Hello ' + item + '!');
        };
}

var hello = new Greeting('world');
hello.log(); // Hello world!
```

 Begin the names of your constructors with a capital letter; this will help you remember whether it is a function or a constructor. This is fairly common practice, so you should be able to recognize constructors in other people's code, too.

It is possible to create the object and call a method on the same line, which can often be useful:

```
new Greeting('alien').log(); // Hello alien!
```

In other languages, the closest thing to constructors are classes. Classes have constructor functions, which in that context are functions that are run when a class is used to create an object. It's easier to specify code that should be run on creation in JavaScript:

```
function Greeting(item) {
        this.item = item;
        console.log('New greeting created.');

        // Do something else here

        this.setItem = function (item) {
                this.item = item;
        };

        this.log = function () {
                console.log('Hello ' + this.item + '!');
        };
}
```

Unlike with classes, there is no way to run some code when the instance is destroyed (sometimes called a deconstructor in other languages, as opposed to the constructor), but you could add something like a .destroy method to the constructor function instead of using the traditional delete keyword to delete objects.

Method Chaining

In jQuery, you may have seen the following syntax used:

```
$('#foo').on('hover', function () {
        // ...
}).on('blur', function () {
        // ...
});
```

This is known as method chaining, as multiple methods are being called one after the other. It is possible to achieve this by using return this at the end of a function, which will return the object so that the function can be run again:

```
function Add(number) {
        if (typeof number !== 'number') {
                number = 0;
        }

        this.add = function (num) {
                number += num;
                return this;
        };
```

```
        this.log = function () {
                console.log(number);
        };
    }
```

We can then call it using the following code:

```
new Add(10).add(5).add(1.5).log(); // 16.5
```

jQuery uses method chaining quite a lot, and it also does so by returning `this`. Considering the first code sample again, we can see that the call to `$('#foo')` `.on('hover')` must return the `$('#foo')` object. We can see this by looking at the jQuery source code; at the bottom of `jQuery.fn.on` is this code:

```
        return this.each( function() {
                jQuery.event.add( this, types, fn, data, selector );
        });
```

`jQuery.fn.each` in turn returns the value of `jQuery.each( this, callback, args )`, which is `this`:

```
        each: function ( object, callback, args ) {
                // ...
                return object;
        },
```

Constructor, Not Function

It is possible to call any function normally, which would result in an error or unexpected behavior if it is a constructor. For example, if we call the last function we defined (Add from the method chaining example) as a normal function, it adds a couple methods to the window object, and then throws a TypeError when we attempt to call the .add method; the Add function doesn't return anything, and undefined has no add method. To work around this, we can simply put the following extract of code at the top of the function:

```
    if (!(this instanceof Add)) {
        return new Add(number);
    }
```

This would make the function perform the same even if you omitted the new constructor. It is fairly bad practice to rely on this, though, and should be avoided.

Another approach would be to throw an error:

```
    if (!(this instanceof Add)) {
        return new Error('This is a constructor, not a function');
    }
```

That would be more useful in a library than in your own code, though (after all, you *know* that functions beginning with capital letters are constructors, right?).

Prototypes

Prototypes allow the developer to create a method or property of an object that is inherited by all instances of that object. For example, look at the following piece of code:

```
function User(id) {
        this.id = id;

        this.sendMsg = function (msg) {
                // Do stuff here
        };

        this.getMsgs = function () {
                // Do stuff here
        };
}
```

Nothing wrong with this code, right? But imagine if we had hundreds, possibly thousands, of that object. Every instance of that object would have a copy of those two functions, which would use quite a bit of memory. If they're exactly the same function on every instance of the object, why do we have to have copies of them instead of reusing the function?

That's exactly what prototypes do. If you add a method to the prototype of the function, then every function will inherit that method. We can rewrite the previous code as the following:

```
function User(id) {
        this.id = id;
}

User.prototype.sendMsg = function (msg) {
        // Do stuff here
};

User.prototype.getMsgs = function (msg) {
        // Do stuff here
};
```

The preceding code would do exactly the same thing, but would use a lot less memory. It also has the advantage that if you edit the prototype of an object after a few of them have been initiated, the existing instances will also use the edited prototype:

```
function User(id) {
        this.id = id;
}

var bob = new User(32);
console.log(bob.foo); // undefined
```

```
User.prototype.foo = 'bar';

console.log(bob.foo); // bar
```

This is because the methods and variables assigned to the prototype aren't copied to the object, but when a method is called it first checks the object for that method, and then the prototype of the object, and then the prototype of the prototype, etc.

If you console.log an object in a good browser, you will be able to inspect the prototype of an object as well as the object itself. Figure 2-1 shows the console.log of an object that was created using var obj = new Constructor(); where Constructor was defined as an empty function. Some properties were then set.

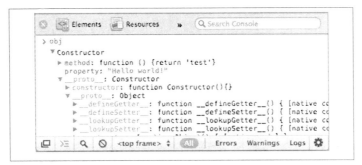

Figure 2-1. console.log to view a prototype

__proto__ is the prototype of the element.

jQuery uses prototypes on jQuery node lists. The $ function can be called hundreds, possibly thousands, of times. If jQuery copied every method and property over every single time, that would be quite costly, and your application would stop doing much very quickly. We assign methods by either calling the jQuery.fn.extend function—which cycles through the given object, adding methods to the prototype—or by adding them directly to jQuery.fn, like so:

```
jQuery.fn.log = function () {
        console.log(this);
        return this;
};
```

We can test that this has worked by running the following code:

```
$('p').log();
```

It should log all the paragraph elements in the document to the console.

The reason that you're adding methods to `jQuery.fn` and not `jQuery.prototype` is that the developers have decided that it looks nicer, and so have added something like the following line of code somewhere:

```
jQuery.fn = jQuery.prototype;
```

As objects are passed by reference and not copied, `jQuery.fn` is equivalent to `jQuery.prototype` and so any modifications to `jQuery.fn` will also be made to the prototype.

.hasOwnProperty

There is a handy function that will tell you whether a method or property is owned by the object or the prototype: `.hasOwnProperty`. For example:

```
var $document = $(document);
$document.log = function () {};

console.log(typeof $document.log); // function
console.log(typeof $document.css); // function; no help here

console.log($document.hasOwnProperty('log')); // true
console.log($document.hasOwnProperty('css')); // false
```

Editing the Prototype of Existing Objects

It is also possible to edit the prototypes of objects that are defined by JavaScript, such as `Array` and `String`. This allows us to add useful methods to them—for example, a method that returns the sum of all the values in an array:

```
Array.prototype.sum = function () {
        for (var sum = 0, i = 0; i < this.length; i++) {
                sum += this[i];
        }

        return sum;
}

console.log([1, 2, 3].sum()); // 6
```

`this` refers to the object that the method is being called from, in this case [1, 2, 3].

The major fundamental difference between jQuery and the Prototype library is that jQuery doesn't touch any prototypes—in fact, it doesn't touch anything except the jQuery and $ variables—and Prototype modifies the prototypes of elements to add functionality to the language instead.

While in theory it is possible to edit the prototypes of objects like NodeList (for example, to add a .forEach function), older versions of Internet Explorer throw an error if you try to access the prototype of an object that isn't one of the five global objects (Array, Boolean, Number, Object, and String). It's also pretty bad practice.

Summary

This chapter has shown you how to create constructor functions and create instances of them using the new keyword, and how you can chain methods by returning this in the method:

```
function Add() {
        var number = 0;
        this.add = function (num) {
                number += num;
        };

        this.getValue = function () {
                return number;
        };
}

new Add().add(4).add(2).add(5).getValue(); // 11
```

We looked at prototypes—how every object inherits methods from the prototype of its constructor function, and the constructor function of that constructor function. We looked at how we can also modify the prototypes of built-in functions to enhance their functionality:

```
Object.prototype.foo = 'bar';
Add.prototype.hello = 'world';

var adder = new Add();

console.log(adder.foo); // bar
console.log(adder.hello); // world
```

Finally, we looked at how we can use the .hasOwnProperty method to see whether a method or property belongs to an object, or the prototype of an object.

CHAPTER 3

DOM Traversal and Manipulation

The Document Object Model (DOM for short) is the API provided by the browser to enable you to view and interact with objects (such as elements) in HTML and XML documents. jQuery includes a number of functions that make working with the DOM a lot easier than with JavaScript alone, which can be pretty ugly. However, the functions provided by jQuery can be rather hefty (especially in older browsers), and it is often a lot faster to just use pure JavaScript. Therefore, it is important to know how both work.

Selecting an Element

In jQuery, there is only really one way to select an element, and that is with the CSS selector:

```
$('#foo');
```

In JavaScript, there are several ways. You can select elements with their CSS selector (which I will cover later), but it isn't supported in Internet Explorer versions earlier than 8, so I will cover the traditional methods first.

You can select an element by its Id, ClassName, or TagName. The syntax is pretty similar for all of them:

```
document.getElementById('foo');
document.getElementsByClassName('bar');
document.getElementsByTagName('p');
```

The first line, document.getElementById, gets the element with ID foo. As there can only be one element associated with each ID, there is no need to return a NodeList here, and it will return either the element or null.

The second line, document.getElementsByClassName, gets all elements with "bar" as one of their classes. It will return the elements as a NodeList, which is similar to an array, as detailed later.

The final line, document.getElementsByTagName, gets all paragraph elements and returns them as a NodeList.

A NodeList is an object that acts like an array, but isn't. This means that you can access the elements using elements[i], but you cannot directly use array methods like .splice and .forEach. You can, however, use them with the Array prototype:

```
var elements = document.getElementsByClassName('bar');
Array.prototype.slice.call(elements, 2, 5);
```

The .slice call will return an array of elements, not a NodeList. This can also be used to convert NodeLists to arrays:

```
var elements = document.getElementsByClassName('bar');
console.log(Array.isArray(elements)); // false

elements = Array.prototype.slice.call(elements);
console.log(Array.isArray(elements)); // true
```

 If you're using a decent browser, then you can probably log elements to the console using console.log. This allows you to see which elements you have selected, and see what you can do with them next.

Selecting Elements with a CSS Selector

It is possible to select elements using CSS selectors via .querySelector and .query SelectorAll:

```
document.querySelector('#foo');
document.querySelectorAll('.bar');
document.querySelectorAll('.bar span, #foo');
document.querySelectorAll('a[href*="danger"]');
```

As demonstrated in the last example, it is possible to use CSS3 selectors (that will select all anchor elements with the word *danger* anywhere in their href). This isn't supported in Internet Explorer, though—Internet Explorer only supports CSS2 selectors, and IE7 and below don't support this function at all.

When only making simple selections such as selecting a single element by ID or selecting some elements by class, it is far more efficient to use the traditional method of selecting them. See a benchmark here: *http://jsperf.com/getelementbyid-vs-jquery-id.*

The Prototype and MooTools libraries have aliases for document.querySelector and document.querySelectorAll: the $ and $$ functions. In addition to being aliases, they add support for browsers that do not support the functions natively (you can use a library such as Sizzle for this):

```
if (!document.querySelector || !document.querySelectorAll) {
        // Load library here
}

function $(selector) {
        return document.querySelector
                ? document.querySelector(selector)
                : customQuerySelector(selector);
}

function $$(selector) {
        return document.querySelectorAll
                ? document.querySelectorAll(selector)
                : customQuerySelectorAll(selector);
}
```

Selecting Children

Sometimes you may want to select the children of an element. With jQuery, this is again very easy:

```
$('#foo').children('.bar')
```

It's also fairly easy in JavaScript, as it is possible to use the .getElement... and .querySelector functions on elements, as well as the document:

```
document.getElementById('foo').getElementsByClassName('bar');
```

Make sure that you don't attempt to run any of them on a NodeList, though—it won't work. Instead, you must loop through the elements. These functions only work on elements:

```
// Does not work:
document.getElementsByTagName('p').getElementsByClassName('test');

// This works:
var elements = document.getElementsByTagName('p'),
        allElements = [];

Array.prototype.forEach.call(elements, function (element) {
        children = element.getElementsByClassName('test');
        allElements = allElements.concat(Array.prototype.slice.call(children));
});

// This also works:
document.querySelectorAll('p .test');
```

Selecting the Next Element

To select the next sibling of an element in jQuery, all we have to do is call the `.next` function:

```
$('#foo').next('.bar');
```

That would return #foo's next sibling with the classname bar. To do this with Java-Script alone is a bit more complicated, but we can do so by using `.nextElementSibling` and a loop, like this:

```
var element = document.getElementById('foo');
element = element.nextElementSibling;
while (element && element.className.indexOf('bar') === -1) {
        element = element.nextElementSibling;
}
```

In the loop, we check whether `element` is truthy, and if it isn't, then we have reached the end of the list and there is no such element. If that is the case, then we break out of the loop and `element` will be null. Then, we check that the element has the class bar; if it doesn't, then we continue the loop. If it matches, then we break out of the loop and `element` contains the element we were looking for. If we don't want to match a selector, we can just use the `.nextElementSibling` property without the while loop (although you might still want to check that it exists).

To find the previous element, you can use similar code, but with `.previousElementSibling`. To find a parent element (`.parent` using jQuery), we can use `.parentElement`.

To return all of an element's siblings (like jQuery's `.siblings`), you have to find the children of the parent element (`.parentNode.childNodes`) and then loop through, removing all nodes that aren't elements, and removing the original element itself; obviously, an element cannot be its own sibling. We can use the following code:

```
var element = document.getElementById('foo');
var elements = element.parentNode.childNodes;

for (var siblings = [], i = 0; i < elements.length; i++) {
    if (elements[i].nodeType === 1 && elements[i] !== element) {
        siblings.push(elements[i]);
    }
}

console.log(siblings);
```

We're using `.push`, as it is more efficient in this case. Converting a NodeList to an array effectively uses `.push` on every element, and then using `.splice` would do some additional work on top of that; it is more efficient to cycle through, running `.push` for all the elements we want.

Creating an Element

Creating an element in jQuery is fairly simple, while it is pretty overcomplicated in JavaScript. Here is how to create an element in jQuery:

```
$('<strong class="test">text</strong>').appendTo('body');
```

There are two ways to create elements in JavaScript. One of them is to modify the `.innerHTML` of the element, but this should usually be avoided as it converts the element (in this case, the body) into HTML, adds the new HTML, and parses it back again. This means that any event listeners and formatting added on the fly will be lost. The other way—the correct way, in this context—is to create the element using `docu ment.createElement`, and then append it using `.appendChild`:

```
// The wrong way, using innerHTML:
document.body.innerHTML += '<strong class="test">text</strong>';

// The correct way:
var newElement = document.createElement('strong');
newElement.setAttribute('class', 'test');
newElement.innerHTML = 'text';
document.body.appendChild(newElement);
```

Using `document.createElement` is longer and more complicated than adjusting the `.innerHTML`, but it is far more efficient. The `.setAttribute` method is fairly descriptive; it sets the `class` attribute to `test` (we could also have used the `.class Name` attribute for this). You may have noticed that I used `.innerHTML` to set the text of the element; in this case, it is fine to change the HTML directly, as it is a blank element and thus it has no additional overhead beyond having to parse what you're passing to it, which isn't much. The alternative to modifying the `.innerHTML` would be to use `document.createTextNode` and append it to `newElement` using the `newEle ment.appendChild` method:

```
var newElement = document.createElement('strong');
newElement.setAttribute('class', 'test');

var text = document.createTextNode('text');
newElement.appendChild(text);

document.body.appendChild(newElement);
```

Both are equally correct, but the first is shorter and more readable.

Modifying an Existing Element

If we want to modify the text of an element in jQuery (say, we want to replace all instances of the word *swear* with *), then we can use the following code:

```
$('#foo').text($('#foo').text().replace(/swear/g, '*****'));
```

That only works on elements with no children; if you run it on an element with children, the child will be removed:

```
<p id="foo">this <b>is</b> a <i>test</i> for <u>swears</u></p>

<!-- After jQuery code has been ran: -->

<p id="foo">this is a test for *****s</p>
```

If we wanted to replace some text on an element with children, we would have to use .html instead of .text. This isn't good, and is effectively the same as this Java-Script:

```
var element = document.getElementById('foo');
element.innerHTML = element.innerHTML.replace(/swear/g, '*****');
```

If the element has a lot of children, then this can be very inefficient, as it has to convert the entire tree to HTML, and then back again when it has been modified. Also, if any element has something like a className of swear, it will be replaced; you may want this behavior, but for the purposes of demonstration, we do not. A better solution would be to cycle through all the children of the element, checking what type it is. If it is a TextNode, then we run the swear regex, and if it is an element then we recurse, running the function again on that element:

```
var TEXT_NODE = 3,
        ELEMENT_NODE = 1;

function replace(element, find, replacement) {
        var child, i, value,
                children = element.childNodes;

        for (i = 0; i < children.length; i++) {
                child = children[i];
                value = child.nodeValue;
                if (child.nodeType === TEXT_NODE) {
                        child.nodeValue = value.replace(find, replacement);
                } else if (child.nodeType === ELEMENT_NODE) {
                        replace(child, find, replacement);
                }
        }
}

var element = document.getElementById('foo');
replace(element, /swear/g, '*****');
```

In the first two lines of this example, we define two constants, TEXT_NODE and ELEMENT_NODE. The reasoning behind this isn't strictly relevant to the example, as we could have just used child.nodeType === 3, but using the constants makes the code more readable; after all, who has memorized all the values for nodeType?

While it is possible to use a string in the `.replace` call, it will be converted to a regex using new `RegExp('swear')`, and so won't be global, meaning that only the first instance of *swear* will be replaced.

Cycling Through Elements

Cycling through elements can be useful for, say, adding an event listener to each of them individually or changing an attribute. In jQuery, cycling through a list of elements is easy:

```
$('.bar').each(function () {
        $(this).css('color', 'red');
});
```

It is also quite easy in JavaScript:

```
var elements = document.getElementsByClassName('bar');
for (var i = 0; i < elements.length; i++) {
        elements[i].style.color = 'red';
}
```

If you want to refer to the element as `this`, you can use an anonymous function with `.call` to set the scope:

```
var elements = document.getElementsByClassName('bar');
for (var i = 0; i < elements.length; i++) {
        (function () {
                this.style.color = 'red';
        }).call(elements[i]);
}
```

It's overkill to do that to merely change the color of a number of elements, but with larger changes it can be a lot cleaner than calling `elements[i]` every single time, and cleaner than assigning the element to a variable at every iteration of the loop (plus we could have the "last one only" problem—detailed in Chapter 5—if we added an event listener, which this approach solves without requiring an additional closure).

Moving and Copying Elements

It can be useful to be able to move and copy elements; for example, we may want to move a `textarea` to another point on a page when a button is pressed. We're talking about moving the element in the DOM here, not necessarily on the page—the latter can be achieved relatively trivially using CSS. In jQuery, we can use the following methods to move and copy elements:

```
$('#foo').insertBefore($('#bar')); // moves #foo to directly before #bar
$('#foo').clone().insertAfter($('#bar')); // copies #foo to after #bar
```

To move an element in pure JavaScript, we can use the `.insertBefore` method:

```
var foo = document.getElementById('foo');
var bar = document.getElementById('bar');
bar.parentNode.insertBefore(foo, bar);
```

`.insertBefore` uses a slightly strange syntax. You have to call it on the parent node, and send the element to insert (`elementToInsert`) and the element to insert it before (`insertBeforeThis`) as arguments (in that order):

```
element.parentNode.insertBefore(elementToInsert, insertBeforeThis);
```

To copy the element, we can simply call the `.cloneNode` method before calling insertBefore:

```
var foo = document.getElementById('foo').cloneNode(true);
var bar = document.getElementById('bar');
bar.parentNode.insertBefore(foo, bar);
```

The argument being passed to `.cloneNode` (`true` in the previous example) should almost always be `true`. It tells JavaScript that you want to clone the entire tree (the children of the element), as well as the element itself. Setting this to `false` or omitting the argument entirely would just copy the children without cloning them, so making any changes to the children of the new element would change the children of the old element (and vice versa).

Summary

In this chapter, we have explored the Document Object Model and how you, the developer, can interact with it using JavaScript in the following ways:

- Selecting elements using the traditional `document.getElement` functions
- Selecting elements using the newer `document.querySelector` functions using CSS selectors
- Selecting children and sibling elements
- Creating elements using `document.createElement`
- Modifying elements using `.innerHTML` and by cycling through them
- Cycling through elements
- Moving and copying elements using `.insertBefore` and `.cloneNode`

CHAPTER 4

AJAX

One of jQuery's most used features is its suite of AJAX functions. They offer some significant improvements over the native JavaScript AJAX features, as they are a lot easier to use. AJAX is the act of making an HTTP request from JavaScript without having to reload the page; you could think of it as an inline HTTP request. Sometimes, however, it isn't worth loading the entire jQuery library to send a few requests and nothing else, or it doesn't provide enough control. It's also useful to know how jQuery does it, as it can help you when you're trying to debug your code. jQuery's $.ajax function is also a massive 379 lines long at the time of writing.

In this chapter, we will cover the basics of AJAX, explore a bit about designing a website to use AJAX, and then AJAXify an example piece of code. This chapter contains a bit of PHP, but PHP knowledge isn't strictly necessary—it's not complicated PHP and I will be explaining it along the way.

Sending an AJAX Request

To send an AJAX request in jQuery, we use this very simple syntax:

```
$.get('/ajax/?foo=bar', function (data) {
        console.log(data); // The response
});
```

Sending an AJAX request in JavaScript alone is a lot more complicated. To send an AJAX request, we use the XMLHttpRequest object (or ActiveXObject in older versions of Internet Explorer). Here is an example of a basic AJAX request:

```
if (window.XMLHttpRequest) {
        var req = new XMLHttpRequest();
} else {
        // Internet Explorer
        var req = new ActiveXObject('Microsoft.XMLHTTP');
```

```
        }

        var url = '/ajax/?foo=bar';

        req.open('GET', url, true);

        req.onreadystatechange = function () {
                if (req.readyState === 4 && req.status === 200) {
                        console.log(req.responseText);
                } else if (req.readyState === 4) {
                        throw new Error('XHR Request failed: ' + req.status);
                }
        };

        req.send();
```

That sends a GET request to *ajax/?foo=bar*, and then if the request succeeds, logs the output to the console. If it fails, it throws an error. There are a few things that you should know about this example:

- The third argument of `req.open` should always be set to `true`, as it tells the browser that you want to make the request asynchronous (runs in the background and then calls the callback, as opposed to blocking the page until the request returns). If set to `false`, it tells the browser that you want a synchronous request. This used to cause a memory leak in Firefox, so Mozilla disabled it; attempting to send a request synchronously now just throws an error. It was also bad practice to use it when it did work.

- It is safe to use `.onreadystatechange` instead of adding an event listener, as we know that only one event listener will be added to it and nothing will be over-written.
  It isn't worth the hassle of adding support for both `.addEventListener` and `.attachEvent`.

- `req.readyState` will always be set to 4, eventually. There is no need to have a `setTimeout` to throw an error on timeout.

- When sending GET requests, you should just append any data you want to send to the end of the URL (like you would for a normal HTTP request). We'll cover POST requests in a bit.

Debugging

For debugging AJAX requests, it is wise to have a simple echo script installed to which you can send data. Mine is written in PHP, but it doesn't matter what language it is written in:

```php
<?php

echo json_encode(array(
        'method'          => $_SERVER['request_method'],
        'GET'             => $_GET,
        'POST'            => $_POST
));

?>
```

That sample of code simply sends a JSON-encoded array of information: first, it sends the request method (usually GET or POST, but DELETE and PUT are also fairly common), and then it dumps the GET ($_GET) and POST ($_POST) information. This allows us to see exactly what has been sent. We can use JSON.parse to turn it into a JavaScript object when we receive it at the client side.

JSON (JavaScript Object Notation) is a unified format for sending data with either native support or libraries written for almost every language. It was pioneered by Douglas Crockford, who also wrote JSLint and JSCheck. In JavaScript, we can use JSON.stringify to turn it into JSON, or JSON.parse to turn it back into a real JavaScript object. It and XML are the most commonly used formats for sending data over AJAX requests, although JSON tends to be more popular recently. I prefer JSON, as it offers better support and uses less bandwidth. Most APIs offer both XML and JSON.

Debugging Sent AJAX Requests

Most good browsers have an option in the console (usually accessible by right-clicking) that, when enabled, will display all AJAX requests in the console. It can be helpful for seeing whether a request has actually been sent, and whether the problem is on the client side or server side.

Some browsers will also log the returned data when this option is enabled, which can be helpful, as well.

Sending POST Requests in JavaScript

The syntax to send a POST request is mostly the same as that to send a GET request, with a couple of minor differences. The following code sends the same data to the same URL as this chapter's first code example, but using POST instead of GET:

```javascript
if (window.XMLHttpRequest) {
        var req = new XMLHttpRequest();
} else {
        // Internet Explorer
        var req = new ActiveXObject('Microsoft.XMLHTTP');
}
```

```
var url = '/ajax/';
var data = 'foo=bar';

req.open('POST', url, true);

req.setRequestHeader('Content-type', 'application/x-www-form-urlencoded');

req.onreadystatechange = function () {
        if (req.readyState === 4 && req.status === 200) {
                console.log(req.responseText);
        } else if (req.readyState === 4) {
                throw new Error('XHR Request failed: ' + req.status);
        }
};

req.send(data);
```

Data is sent using the same format as a query string, but is sent in `req.send`, not as part of the URL. When sending data, we also set the `Content-type` header to `appli cation/x-www-form-urlencoded`.

Writing a Wrapper Function

Instead of writing out a large block of code every time you want to send an AJAX request, we can use a function that will accept arguments such as method, URL, data, and a callback:

```
function request(method, url, data, callback) {
        if (window.XMLHttpRequest) {
                var req = new XMLHttpRequest();
        } else {
                // Internet Explorer
                var req = new ActiveXObject('Microsoft.XMLHTTP');
        }

        if (method === 'GET' && typeof data === 'string') {
                url += '?' + data;
        }

        req.open(method, url, true);

        if (method === 'POST' && typeof data === 'string') {
                req.setRequestHeader('Content-type',
                        'application/x-www-form-urlencoded');
        }

        req.onreadystatechange = function () {
                if (req.readyState === 4 && req.status === 200) {
                        var contentType = req.getResponseHeader('Content-type');
                        if (contentType === 'application/json') {
                                callback(JSON.parse(req.responseText));
```

```
                    } else {
                            callback(req.responseText);
                    }
            } else if (req.readyState === 4) {
                    throw new Error('XHR Request failed: ' + req.status);
            }
    };
    req.send((typeof data === 'string' && method === 'POST') ? data : null);
    return req;
}
```

You can call it using the following code:

```
request('GET', '/ajax', 'foo=bar', function (body) {
        console.log(body);
});
```

You may have noticed that the function includes some code that the original two samples did not; if the Content-type is set to application/json, it attempts to parse it. jQuery does this, too; it's pretty useful.

You could also create some alias functions, like jQuery does:

```
function get(url, data, callback) {
        return request('GET', url, data, callback);
}

function post(url, data, callback) {
        return request('POST', url, data, callback);
}
```

A Simple Application of AJAX

To demonstrate an application of AJAX, we will build a simple page that gets the time from the server. First we will build it without AJAX, and then we will add AJAX support (I'll explain why I did it in that order in a bit).

Let's call our page *ajax.php*, and put the following in it:

```
<!DOCTYPE html>
<html>
<head>
        <title>time()</title>
        <meta charset="utf-8">
</head>
<body>
        <strong>The time() is:</strong>
        <span id="time"><?php echo time(); ?></span>
</body>
</html>
```

As we reload the page, it will update. However, what if we want to update it using a button or automatically? We could use a button to refresh the page, or we could use AJAX. First, we will need to check whether the request is an AJAX request, and then if it is AJAX we will return only the value of time(). Save this as *ajaxUpdate.php*:

```php
<?php

if ($_SERVER['HTTP_X_REQUESTED_WITH'] === 'XMLHttpRequest') {
        echo time();
} else {
        echo 'Please go to ajax.php and request this page using AJAX.';
}

?>
```

This checks whether the request is an AJAX request, and if so it outputs the time. If not, it displays an error to the user. Then we can add the following code to the client side, in order to send the AJAX request:

```javascript
function updateTime() {
        get('ajaxUpdate.php', '', function (time) {
                document.getElementById('time').innerHTML = time;
        });
}
```

Whenever updateTime is called, it sends a request to the server, and when it gets a reply it updates the element to display the updated time value. So the final *ajax.php* is as follows (use it with the original *ajaxUpdate.php*):

```html
<!DOCTYPE html>
<html>
<head>
        <title>time()</title>
        <meta charset="utf-8">
<body>
        <strong>The time() is:</strong>
        <span id="time"><?php echo time(); ?></span>
        <button>Update time</button>

        <!-- functions.js should contain the get
                and addEventListener functions -->
        <script src="functions.js"></script>
        <script>
                var button = document.getElementsByTagName('button')[0];
                addEventListener(button, 'click', function () {
                        get('ajaxUpdate.php', '', function (time) {
                                document.getElementById('time').innerHTML = time;
                        });
                });
        </script>
</body>
</html>
```

Designing a Site with AJAX

There are two approaches to writing an AJAX-enabled website. The first is to write the AJAX to begin with, and the second is to design the entire site without AJAX and then add AJAX afterward. There are several advantages and disadvantages of each approach.

Advantages of the first approach:

- Easier and faster to develop, as it only requires one method to be developed instead of an AJAX and a non-AJAX approach
- Better support for modern browsers
- More freedom, as you can use modern features without having to worry about older browsers

Advantages of the second approach:

- Easier to keep JavaScript and HTML separate, as the HTML doesn't rely on JavaScript
- Better support for older browsers and browsers with JavaScript disabled (which is surprisingly common)

Summary

In this shorter chapter, we looked at AJAX: using the `XMLHttpRequest` object (or `ActiveXObject` in IE) to send both GET and POST requests, as well as using `req.on readystatechange` to get the data that the server sends back. I also explained a couple of ways you can debug sent AJAX requests, and I gave you a wrapper function that you can use to send requests without writing out a huge block of code every time.

Finally, we looked at how we could add AJAX to a simple application, and covered a couple of different approaches to AJAXify applications.

CHAPTER 5

JavaScript Conventions

This chapter will cover some common conventions that you can use to improve your JavaScript. It covers topics such as making your code more readable by using comments and whitespace correctly, optimizing your code in order to improve performance, design patterns, and some common *antipatterns* (code that causes more problems than it solves).

Following the conventions in this chapter will significantly improve the performance and maintainability of your code, and you will find that both the quality of your code and your coding abilities will significantly improve.

Writing JavaScript

It is important when writing JavaScript to make your code as easy to read as possible. This makes your code easier to review, and easier to read back later (say, a couple of years down the road, when your project suddenly gains in popularity and a few bugs are found). It also means that if a developer wants to contribute to your project, or your project is passed on to another developer, that he can read and understand your code without having to study it for a long time beforehand.

Comments

By leaving comments in your code, you are ensuring that anyone who reads your code in the future will be able to tell what it does without having to dissect it. I generally leave comments before every function and at every line or block of code where it isn't immediately clear what it does.

A good example would be this:

```
var i = 0;
while (true) { // Infinite loop until break is called
        console.log(i);
        i++;

        if (i == 6) {
                break;
        }
}
```

The comments before functions generally have a special syntax. They are commonly called *DocBlocks*, and there are applications designed to parse them and create documentation from them. DocBlocks usually follow this general syntax:

```
/**
 * Description of function.
 *
 * @param type name Description of parameter.
 * @param int iterations This is an example.
 * @returns type Description of return value.
 */
function functionName() {
        // Do stuff here
}
```

It shouldn't go any more than a certain amount of characters wide—usually 79, as that is the maximum width of a terminal. You can simply wrap the lines, like this:

```
/**
 * Longer description of function here, wrapping multiple lines. The
 * function does this, this, this, and this.
 *
 * @param int iterations This is an example.
 * @returns type Description of return value.
 */
function functionName() {
        // Do stuff here
}
```

The items that are available depend on the documentation generator you're using, but common ones include those listed in Table 5-1.

Table 5-1. Items available in DocBlocks

Item	Description
@author	Gives the author of the component.
@constructor	Marks the function as a constructor.
@deprecated	Marks the function as deprecated.
@description	Some documentation parsers prefer @description to putting the description on the first line.
@example	Shows an example code snippet.
@extends	Says what the function or object extends (doesn't really apply much to JavaScript, but it is good to know).
@ignore	Tells the documentation to ignore the block of code following the comment.
@link	Links to another class or function in the documentation (@sometag See here: {@link MyFunc tion}).
@namespace	Give the name of the namespace where the function resides.
@param	Describes a parameter of the function. Replaces @argument, which is deprecated.
@private	Marks the function as private, and it will not be shown in the documentation.
@public	Marks the opposite of @private, and implied if not specified.
@returns	Describes what the function returns.
@see	Says to see another function (@see MyFunction).
@since	Says what version the function was added in.
@throws	Says that the function may throw this error.
@version	Gives the version number of the file or class.

I've written a longer example containing multiple DocBlocks. As well as the DocBlocks before the comments that we have seen before, it also contains a DocBlock at the very beginning of the file to explain what the file does, and some basic info such as a version number and author information. This would also be where you'd put a copyright and license. The following code sample would be included into another project as a library:

```
/**
 * parser.js: Parses some text.
 *
 * @version 1.0.2
 * @author Callum Macrae <callum@lynxphp.com>
 */

/**
 * Parses some text.
 *
 * @constructor
 * @example
 *   var textParse = new Parser();
 *   textParse.parse(text);
 *   textParse.get('name');
 * @since 1.0.0
```

```
   */
function Parser() {
        this.data = {};
}

/**
 * Parses the text given to it.
 *
 * @param string text The string to parse.
 * @returns object The parser object you called.
 * @since 1.0.1
 */
Parser.prototype.parse = function (text) {
        // Parse text...
        return this;
};

/**
 * The old function to add text to parse.
 * Replaced with .parse: {@link Parser.prototype.parse}
 *
 * Will be removed completely in the near future.
 *
 * @deprecated
 * @see Parser.prototype.parse
 */
Parser.prototype.addText = function () {
        return this.parse.call(this, arguments);
};

/**
 * Gets some parsed data.
 *
 * @param string item The item to return.
 * @returns string The item specified by the item
 *   argument. If not found, will return null.
 * @since 1.0.0
 */
Parser.prototype.get = function (item) {
        return this.data[item];
};
```

Coding Standards

It is important to maintain good and consistent standards while coding. This, as I said before, is advantageous for multiple reasons—mostly because it is easier to read, both by yourself at a later date and by others.

Whitespace

The easiest and best way to make your code easier to read is to use whitespace (both tabs and spaces). I'll give you a few examples of how I use whitespace:

```
// Calling functions

functionName('test',[1,2,3]);             // Not enough whitespace
functionName('test', [1, 2, 3]);          // Just right
functionName ( 'test ' , [ 1 , 2 , 3 ] ); // Too much


// Declaring variables

var a='foo',b='bar';     // Not enough
var a = 'foo',
    b = 'bar';           // Just right (although it could be on one line, too)


// If statements, while statements, etc.

if(foo){
      // Do stuff
}else{
      // Do other stuff
}

// Better:
if (foo) {
      // Do stuff
} else {
      // Do other stuff
}


// Indents

if (foo) {
console.log('test'); // Needs indenting!
}

if (foo) {
      console.log('test');
}
```

As you can see in all those examples, the ones with more whitespace are more readable than the ones without. Too much whitespace, however, can have the same effect as not enough whitespace, and make the code tricky to read.

Curly braces

Curly braces are used to denote either object literals or block statements, the latter of which group statements together as follows:

```
{
        statement_1();
        statement_2();
}
```

Curly braces are usually used with control flow statements such as if and while:

```
if (comparison) {
        statement_1();
        statement_2();
}
```

This control statement simply runs the statement directly after it, and the block statement has nothing to do with the if statement. In fact, the block statement is entirely optional, as you can see here:

```
if (comparison)
        statement_1;
```

However, because the control statement only runs the statement following it, if you decide at a later date to add another statement, you will need to add the curly braces. For that reason, I tend to just use the curly braces at all times, even when there is only one statement (it looks better, too).

The topic of where to put curly braces is, in most languages, a bit of a holy war. The two usual contenders are braces on the same line:

```
if (test) {
        // Do something
} else {
        // Do something else
}
```

Or on their own line:

```
if (test)
{
        // Do something
}
else
{
        // Do something else
}
```

Both make sense, both look fairly good, and both work. However, there are still some cases where the braces must go on the same line (for example, when you're declaring an object). Also, anonymous functions don't look good with the braces on their own line:

```
// Excerpt
someFunction('test', function ()
{
      // Do something
});
```

For this reason, a lot of developers who usually put braces on their own line (usually because they're not primarily JavaScript developers) put the braces for anonymous functions on the same line. This can result in samples of code like the following, which doesn't look good at all:

```
var obj = {
      test: function () {
            for (var i = 0; i < arguments.length; i++)
            {
                  if (typeof arguments[i] === 'string')
                  {
                        handleString(arguments[i], function () {
                              return {
                                    foo: 'bar';
                              };
                        });
                  }
                  else
                  {
                        handleOther(arguments[i]);
                  }
            }
      }
};
```

It's inconsistent and messy, and the reason that I recommend that you put the braces on the same line in all cases.

Naming conventions

Inconsistent naming conventions make it difficult to remember and work out variable names. While there isn't really a wrong way to name variables, it is very important that you keep them consistent. Here are the most common ways of naming variables and functions:

```
// Camel caps
var thisVarName = '';
function myFunction() {}

// Underscores
var this_var_name = '';
function my_function() {}

// All lowercase
var thisvarname = '';
function myfunction() {}
```

```
// Underscores with capitals
var This_Var_Name = '';
function My_Function() {}
```

JavaScript itself uses the first—camel caps—in its native functions. For this reason, code that uses camel caps tends to look better than code that uses a different naming convention, and camel caps tend to be most widely used. The second convention demonstrated, underscores, is also pretty commonly used, but isn't as popular in JavaScript as it is in some other languages.

Throughout this book, I have been using camel caps.

Literals Notation

JavaScript has literal notations available for stuff like creating new objects and arrays, which allow you to shorten your code and make it clearer. It is better to use literals than the constructor functions, such as `new Object()` and `new Array()`, and I'll explain why using a few examples.

Object Literals

The object literal simply uses curly braces. Here are two ways of defining exactly the same object:

```
// Using the literal syntax
var obj = {};

// Using the constructor function (antipattern)
var obj = new Object();
```

The most obvious reason to use the literal syntax instead of the constructor function is that it is shorter to type, but there are a couple more reasons. The literal syntax never has scoping issues—if, for example, you accidentally call a variable `Object`, you would overwrite the object constructor, and you would not be able to create any more objects using the constructor function. This can never happen to the literal syntax. In a similar vein, the parser doesn't have to do any scope resolution with the literal syntax. If you use the literal syntax, JavaScript knows exactly what you mean and gives you an object. If you use the constructor function, however, then JavaScript has to check the current scope, then cycle up through the parent scopes until it finds the `Object` constructor. The first uses fewer resources and is slightly quicker. Finally, you can declare properties using the literal notation:

```
// Using the literal syntax
var obj = {
        foo: 'bar',
        hello: 'world'
};
```

```
// Using the constructor function (antipattern)
var obj = new Object();
obj.foo = 'bar';
obj.hello = 'world';
```

Other Literals

Sometimes the constructor offers features that the literal does not, and so the constructor should be used. For example, with `Array` objects, you can send an integer argument to the constructor, and it will specify the length of the array. This can be useful for repeating a string:

```
var repeats = 6;
var str = 'test ';
str = New Array(repeats + 1).join(str);
console.log(str); // test test test test test test
```

Unlike the literal, the `RegExp` constructor accepts string input, so you can concatenate user input into it (which you cannot do with the literal):

```
var re = new RegExp('\nUser: ' + username + '\n', 'g');
```

Table 5-2 lists constructors and their corresponding literals.

Table 5-2. Constructors and literals

Constructors	Literals
var obj = new Object();	var obj = {};
var ary = new Array();	var ary = [];
var re = new RegExp('[a-z]+', 'g');	var re = /[a-z]+/g
var str = new String();	var str = '';
var num = new Number();	var num = 0;
var bool = new Boolean();	var bool = false;

Optimizations

Optimizing your code can make it faster and use fewer resources. A *micro-optimization*, which I will demonstrate in this section, is an optimization that improves the performance of the script by a negligible (not noticeable) amount. When you're running an application on a server, improving the performance of a script by a couple of microseconds can improve the application's overall performance by reducing the response time of the server by a couple of microseconds per request, freeing it up for other requests. However, on the client side, micro-optimizations are less important because the user won't notice a few microseconds' difference.

Strictly speaking, micro-optimizations should be the job of the browser. However, not all browsers have fast JavaScript engines, and some people would argue that the day when micro-optimizations are no longer necessary is not yet here.

However, it is important to know a few of the most effective micro-optimizations for JavaScript; if you're writing code that could be used on the server side or on very old browsers, micro-optimizations could help.

To read about optimizing your code in far more detail than I could fit into a section of a chapter, check out *High Performance JavaScript* (*http://oreil.ly/High_Perfor mance_js*) by Nicholas C. Zakas.

Algorithms

The easiest and most efficient way of speeding up your script and lowering resource usage is to design your algorithms more efficiently. For example, if you're implementing a sorting algorithm to order some elements and you're comparing every element with every other element, why not just compare it to the nearest ones? This area is more algorithm design than JavaScript, so I won't be covering it here.

This type of optimization doesn't usually count as a micro-optimization, as it can often noticeably speed up your script.

Caching Variables

When looping through an array or NodeList, you generally call the `.length` property at every iteration. Every time you read that property, the length has to be calculated, which can be expensive. Instead, you can cache the length in a variable:

```
for (var i = 0, l = ary.length; i < l; i++) {
        // Do something here
}
```

When finding an element using jQuery, you'd be wise to cache it instead of calling the jQuery function multiple times:

```
$('#foo').click(function () {
        $.myFunc($('#foo'), function () {
                $('#foo').show();
        });
        $('#foo').hide();
});

// Better:
var foo = $('#foo');
foo.click(function () {
        $.myFunc(foo, function () {
```

```
            foo.show();
        });
        foo.hide();
    });
```

This is a minor improvement, though, and makes the code slightly harder to read; if you want to know what element a variable contains, you might have to scroll back a bit.

parseInt

parseInt takes a string and returns a parsed number. However, it also contains some additional functionality that you may not need, which will slow the function down. In such a case, you can use new Number(*12*) to convert a string into a number without the additional overhead:

```
parseInt('35'); // 35
new Number('35'); // faster

parseInt('21.8'); // 21
new Number('21.8'); // 21.8

parseInt('3 dogs'); // 3
new Number('3 dogs'); // NaN
```

One thing to bear in mind is that the latter method returns an object, not a number:

```
typeof parseInt('3'); // number
typeof new Number('3'); // object
```

The easiest way to convert the string into an actual number is to precede it with +, the unary operator:

```
typeof +new Number('3'); // number
```

It is worth noting that unless you're going to be using typeof on the number, you don't need to cast it to a number—as soon as you perform an arithmetic operation with the object, it will be treated as a number anyway. This is how we changed the type in the previous example.

Loops

In addition to the preceding code (caching the length), there are other ways to increase the speed of a loop. You can cycle through the loop backward:

```
for (var i = array.length; i--;) {
        // Do something
}
```

As this only runs one statement per loop, it performs twice as well. When i hits zero, the loop will be stopped. Even faster still for this is the while loop:

```
var i = 100;
while (i--) {
        // Do something
}
```

Minimize Repeated Expressions

Instead of repeating the same code multiple times, it is more efficient to store it in a variable. For example:

```
var top = 10 * (x / 7 + y / 5);
var bottom = 5 * (x / 7 + y / 5);
var left = 4 * (x / 7 + y / 5);
var right = 13 * (x / 7 + y / 5);

// Better:
var factor = (x / 7 + y / 5);
var top = 10 * factor;
var bottom = 5 * factor;
var left = 4 * factor;
var right = 13 * factor;
```

Functions

There are multiple conventions involving functions that you can use to improve your code.

Declarations Versus Expressions

Function declarations and function expressions perform in different ways and can be used to complete different tasks. As demonstrated here, there are three types of functions: a declared function, an anonymous function, and a named function. For example:

```
// Function declaration
function test() {
        // Do something
}

// Anonymous function expression
var test = function () {
        // Do something
};

// Named function expression
var test = function test () {
        // Do something
};
```

You may have noticed two slight differences in the coding standards of function expressions and function declarations. As a personal preference only, I have placed a space before the parentheses in the expressions but not the declaration. This is to mark them as function expressions, as it sometimes isn't clear at first glance:

```
(function test () {
        // Do something
}());

test(); // Error; not defined
```

I also put a semicolon after the function expressions, as dumb minifiers prefer it; you can put a function declaration on one line with stuff after it without a semicolon, but a function expression must be followed by a semicolon.

As previously noted, declarations and expressions both perform differently. Much like variables, function declarations are *hoisted* (placed at the beginning of the scope) and so can be called before they're actually defined. For example, the following code works fine (although it doesn't actually do anything):

```
test();
function test() {
        // Do something
}
```

It performs slightly strangely, though; the function will be hoisted even if the block of code will never be run. This can result in weird situations like the following:

```
test(); // false

if (true) {
        function test() {
                return true;
        }
} else {
        console.log('test'); // will never be called
        function test() {
                return false;
        }
}
```

That doesn't happen with anonymous or named function expressions.

Function Callbacks

There are conventions regarding the correct usage of anonymous and named functions as callbacks. The only alternatives to using an anonymous function as a callback are to use setInterval to check whether the function has changed a variable and run some code when it has, or use eval:

```
// Warning: antipattern!
function call(func) {
        eval(func + '()');
}
```

Obviously, that function is dangerous and vulnerable. A slightly better example can be explained using event handling. (The following code isn't actually possible, but imagine that it is for this example.) onEventSetToTrue will set clicked to true when #foo is clicked:

```
var clicked = false;
onEventSetToTrue('#foo', 'click', clicked);

function handler() {
        if (clicked) {
                clicked = false;
                // Do something else
        }
}

setInterval('handler()', 100);
```

This isn't nearly as efficient as just giving it a callback, as there can be a delay. Also, if you click the element more than once in 100 ms, the event handler will only be called once. Even the previous example should have used a callback; we're effectively using eval when we give setInterval a string. It also looks nicer when we use a callback:

```
$('#foo').click(function () {
        // Do something
});
```

If Invoking Self-Defining Functions

A *self-invoking* function is an anonymous function that is defined, and then run straightaway. It is mainly useful for resolving scoping issues:

```
(function () {
        // Do something
})();
```

jQuery plug-ins use it for accessing the jQuery variable as $ without overwriting any existing variable that could have been defined by other libraries, and to prevent pollution of the global namespace:

```
(function ($) {
        // Do something
})(jQuery);
```

Self-invoking functions can also have the parentheses to call the function inside the wrapper parentheses, but it is more common to find them outside:

```
(function () {
        // Do something
}());
```

Self-defining functions use a similar concept, and are good for resolving browser compatibility issues. For example, consider the following code:

```
function matchesSelector(element, selector) {
        if (element.matchesSelector) {
                return element.matchesSelector(selector);
        } else if (element.webkitMatchesSelector) {
                return element.webkitMatchesSelector(selector);
        } else if (element.mozMatchesSelector) {
                return element.mozMatchesSelector(selector);
        }
        // else call a library here
}
```

There are a couple of disadvantages to using this code. Every time the function is called, it has to potentially check a few properties of the element until it finds what it needs, and the library needs to be loaded even if it isn't going to be used. We can use the following code instead, which uses the special kind of self-invoking function known as a self-defining function:

```
var matchesSelector = (function () {
        if (HTMLElement.prototype.matchesSelector) {
                return function (element, selector) {
                        return element.matchesSelector(selector);
                };
        } else if (HTMLElement.prototype.webkitMatchesSelector) {
                return function (element, selector) {
                        return element.webkitMatchesSelector(selector);
                };
        } else if (HTMLElement.prototype.mozMatchesSelector) {
                return function (element, selector) {
                        return element.mozMatchesSelector(selector);
                };
        }
        // Load library here
        return function (element, selector) {
                // Call library here
        };
})();
```

It's quite a bit longer, but it is far more efficient. Not only does the function not need to check what exists every single time despite the fact that it won't ever change, but the function also gives us a convenient place to load the library so that the library will only ever be loaded when it is actually needed.

Code Reuse

It is far harder to maintain code when it is repeating itself. The action of DRYing your code (where DRY is Don't Repeat Yourself) moves repeating code into functions and assigns identical strings to variables. It leads to easier-to-read and easier-to-maintain code, and also reduces the footprint of the code, making it use less bandwidth. Consider the following code sample, which takes a few elements and moves them 10 pixels right and 10 pixels up:

```
$('#foo').css('top', '-=10px');
$('#foo').css('left', '+=10px');
$('#bar').css('top', '-=10px');
$('#bar').css('left', '+=10px');
$('#hello').css('top', '-=10px');
$('#hello').css('left', '+=10px');
$('#world').css('top', '-=10px');
$('#world').css('left', '+=10px');
```

What happens if you decide that you want to move the elements 20 px instead of 10 px? You have to change every value manually. If you have a good code editor, it is easy to change them, but it is better to not have to. You could also use a variable, but that would create some very ugly code:

```
var dist = 10;
$('#foo').css('top', '-=' + dist + 'px');
$('#foo').css('left', '+=' + dist + 'px');
$('#bar').css('top', '-=' + dist + 'px');
$('#bar').css('left', '+=' + dist + 'px');
$('#hello').css('top', '-=' + dist + 'px');
$('#hello').css('left', '+=' + dist + 'px');
$('#world').css('top', '-=' + dist + 'px');
```

It is better to do something like this:

```
['#foo', '#bar', '#hello', '#world'].forEach(function(el) {
        $(el).css('top', '-=10px')
                .css('left', '+=10px');
});
```

Now you only have to change two values. This is far easier to change without making any significant edits; imagine this example over thousands of lines, with hundreds of operations.

Common Antipatterns

In addition to being aware of the common conventions, it is important for you to be aware of the common antipatterns, too. You should actively avoid any of the code that you find in this section.

Using eval

`eval` runs (evaluates) the string given to it as JavaScript code:

```
var code = 'console.log("test");';
eval(code);
```

The preceding code simply logs "test" to the console.

`eval` is used fairly commonly by developers who don't know how to do something without it. For example, the following example is sometimes used to access a property of an object. It is an antipattern, as there is an easier way to do it:

```
var property = 'testProperty';
var value = eval('obj.' + property);

// Preferred:
var value = obj[property];
```

In general, if you're using `eval`, you're doing it wrong.

`eval` is such a problem because it opens up your code to potentially execute unsafe operations. It is generally used to accept input from the user, or receive code from a remote server. If you're receiving data from an external source, you don't know that the data hasn't been tampered with, and thus you could be executing malicious code. If accepting input from the user, you don't need to use `eval`, so you shouldn't.

In addition to passing code to the `eval` function itself, there are other, similar ways of evaluating code from strings that you should avoid. You can pass code to `set Interval` and `setTimeout` in strings, and the `Function` object accepts a string:

```
setInterval('console.log("test")', 1000);
setTimeout('someFunction()', 1000);
new Function('console.log("test")');
```

Don't do that!

with

The `with` statement was designed to offer a shorthand way to access properties of an object. Unfortunately, it doesn't always behave quite as expected and can be confusing, so you should avoid it.

When you attempt to access a variable within a `with` statement, the browser first checks whether the object has that property, and if not, it accesses the variable normally. Consider the following code:

```
with (obj) {
        a = b;
}
```

What does it do? It could be doing any one of the following:

```
a = b
a = obj.b
obj.a = b
obj.a = obj.b
```

Without going back and looking at the object, we have no idea what is happening. It is also slower than accessing the object or variable directly.

document.write

document.write is a function used commonly in tutorials to demonstrate outputting values. Basically, it outputs whatever is given to it:

```
<p>
        <script>document.write('Hello world!');</script>
</p>
```

Output:

```
<p>
        Hello world!
</p>
```

That is (usually) as far as the tutorials take it, besides conditionals and variable output. There is almost no situation where document.write is a useful function to have; for outputting elements, there is document.createElement, and for debugging, there is console.log, which is a far superior function because it supports outputting objects, elements, and functions as well as text, numbers, and Boolean values like docu ment.write. In addition, document.write behaves differently depending on where it is called; if it is called after the document has finished loading, it will entirely overwrite the existing DOM, destroying the page.

Common Design Patterns

Design patterns are conventions that will help you with the design or structure of your code, and can be used on your code to solve a common problem. As many developers have used them before us, you can be fairly sure that these patterns will solve your problem in a clean and efficient way. In this section, I will explain a few of the more common design patterns and how they can be implemented in JavaScript.

This is not a fully comprehensive guide to design patterns in JavaScript. To find out a lot more about this topic, I would recommend *Learning JavaScript Design Patterns* (*http://oreil.ly/js_design_patterns*) by Addy Osmani, which in addition to being published by O'Reilly, is available as a free book online (*http://bit.ly/ZQNe8L*).

The Singleton Pattern

You would implement the Singleton pattern, in other languages, by creating a class with a method that creates a new instance of a class if one doesn't exist, or return that object if it already does. It is used in languages where only the current scope is checked, instead of the current scope and then all the parents.

So, in short, implementing the Singleton pattern is as simple as just creating an object:

```
var demoSingleton = {
        foo: 'bar',
        hello: function () {
                return 'Hello world!';
        }
}
```

There is no need to do anything special.

That hasn't really explained Singleton very well; there is no easy way to explain it in JavaScript. The following information isn't really necessary unless you want to know what the Singleton pattern actually is, so if you aren't interested in that or don't know PHP (which is what I will be using to explain it), you can skip to the next subheading.

The following code sample is bad code, as it uses globals:

```
<?php

class MyClass {
        // ...
}
$myClass = new MyClass();

function myFunction() {
        global $myClass;
        // ...
}
```

It is better to not use globals, so instead we create a static class (which is automatically global) and use it to get the object:

```
<?php

class MyClass {
        // ...
}
class MyClassSingleton {
        private $myClass;
        public static function get() {
                if (!is_object($this->myClass)) {
                        $this->myClass = new MyClass();
                }
                return $this->myClass;
        }
```

```
        }

        function myFunction() {
                $myClass = MyClassSingleton::get();
                // ...
        }
```

$myClass is then an instance of the MyClass object.

The Factory Pattern

The Factory pattern is a creational pattern that helps create objects. It creates a generic interface for creating objects without using a constructor, where we can specify the type of the factory object to be created.

This pattern is easiest to explain by example. We're going to be simulating a real factory in the following code example:

```
        function Ford(options) {
                this.color = options.color || 'blue';
                this.year = options.year || new Date().getFullYear();
        }

        function Mini(options) {
                this.color = options.color || 'red';
                this.model = options.model || 'Cooper';
        }

        function CarFactory(){}
        CarFactory.prototype.carType = Ford; // Default is ford
        CarFactory.prototype.createCar = function (options) {
                if (options.carType === 'mini') {
                        this.carType = Mini;
                } else if (options.carType === 'ford') {
                        this.carType = Ford;
                }

                return new this.carType(options);
        };

        var factory = new CarFactory();
        var mini = factory.createCar({
                carType: 'mini',
                model: 'One'
        });
```

We can then see by logging the mini variable to the console that it is an instance of the Mini object. You can also use instanceof to confirm this.

Another approach would be to have an object telling the .createCar method where all the cars are instead of having an if-else statement. This makes it easier to add other cars, and it also means that cars can be added on the fly. For example:

```
function Ford(options) {
        this.color = options.color || 'blue';
        this.year = options.year || new Date().getFullYear();
}

function Mini(options) {
        this.color = options.color || 'red';
        this.model = options.model || 'Cooper';
}

function CarFactory(){}
CarFactory.prototype.carType = Ford; // Default is ford
CarFactory.prototype.carTypes = {
        ford: Ford,
        mini: Mini
};
CarFactory.prototype.createCar = function (options) {
        if (options.carType && this.carTypes[options.carType]) {
                this.carType = this.carTypes[options.carType];
        }

        return new this.carType(options);
};
```

Be careful where you use the Factory pattern. If the problem doesn't require this pattern, then using it could make your code unnecessarily complicated. It's most useful where initiating the object is complex, or where a lot of small objects need to share the same properties or methods.

The Iterator Pattern

The Iterator pattern is a commonly used design pattern that makes it very easy to iterate through the elements of an aggregate object. For example, consider the following code:

```
var element, elements = new ElementIterator('.foo');
while ((element = elements.next())) {
        console.log(element);
}
```

That code simply loops through all elements with className foo, logging them to the console. What is special, however, is how the code is getting the elements; instead of looping through them with a for loop, we're using a while loop with a call to elementIterator.next. This can have a few advantages over just a for loop, such as the ability to add a .previous method as well as a .next method and go backward and forward as required.

The following is an example implementation of the `ElementIterator` function that would allow the previous code to run:

```
function ElementIterator(selector) {
        this.elements = document.querySelectorAll(selector);
        this.currentElement = -1;
}

ElementIterator.prototype.current = function () {
        return this.elements[this.currentElement];
};

ElementIterator.prototype.hasNext = function () {
        return !!(this.elements[this.currentElement + 1]);
};
ElementIterator.prototype.next = function () {
        if (this.hasNext()) {
                this.currentElement++;
                return this.current();
        } else {
                return undefined;
        }
};
```

The `.next` and `.hasNext` methods can easily be adapted for both `.previous` and `.hasPrevious`. It is also common to see a `.reset` or `.restart` method, which would reset `this.currentElement` to 0 and return the first element.

The Facade Pattern

The final design pattern that I will be covering here is also among the smallest and simplest design patterns. Facade (or sometimes *façade*, the French word from which it originates) means "frontage"; that is, obscuring what goes on underneath with something different.

Basically, a facade function is a function that calls a number of other functions in order to make a process simpler for the user. For example, given two functions, `function1()` and `function2()`, the following is an example of the Facade pattern in action:

```
function functions1and2() {
        function1();
        function2();
}
```

That's simple enough.

The usage of the Facade pattern has a couple of advantages and disadvantages. It makes the code easier to read and is DRYer, but it can hit performance when using this pattern; you've got to consider how significant that performance impact is and whether it is worth it.

In jQuery, `$.fn.css` and `$.fn.animate` are examples of facade functions, as they call multiple internal functions without actually doing much themselves.

Summary

In this chapter, we have explored some common conventions in JavaScript, and how using them can help both your code and your ability to write it. We also explored antipatterns, specifically how they can have a detrimental effect on your code and thus should be avoided. We also looked into a few of the more common design patterns, and how using them can improve the structure of your code.

Here are a few conventions we discussed:

- Comments and DocBlocks.
- Coding standards, such as the use of whitespace, the naming of variables and functions, and the placement of curly braces.
- Literal notations versus using the constructor functions such as `Array` and `Function`.
- Optimizations, including demonstrations of a few micro-optimizations and questioning whether they're really necessary.
- Function declarations versus expressions, the function callback pattern, and self-defining and self-invoking functions.
- The basic concepts of code reuse, and DRYing your code.
- Some common antipatterns, including the use of `eval`, the `with` statement, and `document.write`.

We also covered a few of the most basic design patterns:

- The Singleton pattern (specifically, how it doesn't apply to JavaScript)
- The Factory pattern
- The Iterator pattern
- The Facade pattern

For a longer read on conventions and patterns in JavaScript, try *JavaScript Patterns* (*http://oreil.ly/js_Patterns*) by Stoyan Stefanov.

JavaScript Basics

JavaScript is a versatile, lightweight, and easy-to-use scripting language. It is most often used in websites and web-based applications, although it is becoming increasingly common to find it used on the server side using a server-side implementation of JavaScript such as Node.js (*http://nodejs.org/*). Some desktop and mobile applications are even starting to use JavaScript and HTML5.

Due to the wide usage and huge popularity of JavaScript, many libraries have been written for it, a few of which include jQuery, YUI, Dojo, and MooTools. jQuery is currently the most popular, with 85% of the market share and thousands of contributors. Many major projects are built off jQuery, such as jQuery Mobile, Twitter Bootstrap, and jQuery UI.

It is also extremely fast—Apple and Google's fight for the fastest JavaScript engine (Safari's Nitro and Chrome's V8 engine, respectively) has pushed the engineers at both companies to improve the speed of the engines to the point where micro-optimizations are almost entirely unnecessary.

JavaScript is a very forgiving language, and often developers can make mistakes without them having an effect on the site; browsing the Internet with the JavaScript console open often displays errors on many big websites. Unfortunately, this has the side effect of allowing the developers to make mistakes of which they are not made aware, and they develop bad habits that they may then pass on to other people. A lot of online tutorials, and often even books, contain misleading or incorrect information, and will lead the reader into bad habits.

Hello World!

This appendix is a quick explanation of what you can do in JavaScript, explained mostly from your existing jQuery knowledge. If you're not confident with your JavaScript abilities or only know jQuery, it is definitely worth reading this chapter; while you may know some of the material it covers already, it is definitely good to have it explained properly.

I'll be explaining the basic features of JavaScript, such as strings, functions, and variables, primarily using examples; they're fairly easy to pick up. To display output in this chapter, we will be using the built-in `console.log` function. This simply outputs the arguments passed to it into the browser's JavaScript console. This function doesn't work in IE8 and older versions of Firefox, and will throw an error if you try to use it. Throughout the appendix, I'll be using Google Chrome for examples and demonstrations. You can access the console in Chrome in View → Developer → JavaScript Console (it is also worth getting into the habit of using the keyboard shortcut: Option-Command-I in OS X, or Ctrl-Shift-I in Windows).

For example, the following code logs "Hello World!" to the console, as shown in Figure A-1:

```
console.log('Hello World!'); // Hello World!
```

Figure A-1. "Hello World!" in the console

The "undefined" that you can see in Figure A-1 is the return value of the code that was run, which in this case is `undefined`, as the function didn't return anything. We can also return values to view them, instead of using `console.log`. For an example of that, see Figure A-2.

Figure A-2. "Hello World!" in the console (returned)

We passed a string to `console.log`. You'll probably have used strings in jQuery and in any other programming language you've worked with. A string is just a collection of characters wrapped in quotes (either single or double): `"This is a string"`. Unlike with some other languages, single quotes and double quotes behave exactly the same; it doesn't matter which you use. You can concatenate (join) two strings together using the + operator:

```
console.log('Hello ' + "World!"); // Hello World!
```

The same character is also used to add numbers together (this time, as the unary operator). We'll cover numbers in more detail later:

```
console.log(2 + 3); // 5
```

Comments

Comments are easy in JavaScript, and you have probably already used them when writing jQuery. A comment is simply a note in the code that you can read to refamiliarize yourself when you come back to that code later. The JavaScript engine will ignore it:

```
// This is a comment, and won't be parsed

/* This comment spans
multiple lines
*/
```

Comments are also commonly used to prevent the execution of some code, which can be useful when debugging your code:

```
console.log('one'); // one
//console.log('two'); // will not run
console.log('three'); // three
```

Variables

Variables are also pretty easy. Again, you have likely used them when writing jQuery, but you may have been using them wrong (for example, by not declaring them). You must declare all variables using var. For example:

```
var foo = 'bar';
console.log(foo); // bar
```

Due to the forgiving nature of JavaScript, it won't actually complain if you don't declare the variable, but you may encounter debugging issues because such a variable does not behave the same as one that has been declared.

JavaScript has what is known as a *function scope*, which determines where variables can be accessed from based upon where they were defined. For example, a variable declared within a function will become "local" to that function, which means that it can only be accessed from within that function, or any functions declared within that function. Any variable declared outside a function will become "global," and can be accessed from anywhere, including in functions. For example:

```
var a = 'foo';
function test() {
        var b = 'bar';
        console.log(a); // foo
        console.log(b); // bar
}
test();
console.log(a); // foo
console.log(b); // ReferenceError: undefined
```

In this code sample, we can see that the variable a, defined outside the function, can be accessed from within the function. The variable b can be accessed from within the function, but not outside of the function like a can.

A variable declared outside a function, but modified inside the function without being redeclared, will stay modified:

```
var a = 'foo';
var b = 'bar';
function test() {
        a = 'test';
        var b = 'Hello!';
        console.log(a); // test
        console.log(b); // Hello!
}
test();

console.log(a); // test
console.log(b); // bar
```

This code sample is similar to the previous one, but a is changed—and stays changed. It also shows us that variables declared inside the function that are also declared outside the function do not overwrite the old value, which is still the same after the function has been called.

While some tutorials and websites may tell you that omitting the var declaration is safe and just declares the variable globally, this is very bad practice and should not be done unless the variable has been declared in a parent scope.

Numbers

You can perform arithmetic operations in JavaScript:

```
console.log(2 + 2); // 4
console.log(4 - 2); // 2
console.log(4 * 2); // 8
console.log(6 / 2); // 3
```

We can also use noninteger numbers:

```
console.log(3.5 + -2); // 1.5
console.log(5.75 - 2.2); // 3.55
```

You can use the parseInt and parseFloat functions to convert a string into a number. parseInt ignores anything after the first decimal place, meaning that it will always return a whole number, while parseFloat returns the number exactly as it displays. For example:

```
console.log(parseInt('122')); // 122
console.log(parseInt('1.8')); // 1
console.log(typeof parseInt('122')); // number
console.log(parseFloat('3.5')); // 3.5
console.log(typeof parseFloat('3.5')); // number
```

We can perform some more complicated arithmetic tasks using the built-in Math object:

```
console.log(Math.round(3.4)); // 3
console.log(Math.ceil(3.4)); // 4
console.log(Math.pow(2, 10)); // 1024
```

To see a full list of functions in the Math object, you can consult the documentation at the MDN website (*http://mzl.la/Wyiani*).

The Assignment Operators

When working with a variable that has a numeric value, you can use the following shortcuts to modify the value:

```
var x = 2;
x += 7; // x = x + 9 (9)
x -= 1; // x = x - 1 (8)
x *= 2; // x = x * 2 (16)
x /= 4; // x = x / 4 (4)
```

As a further shortcut, there are operators for incrementing and decrementing a variable by one. They're the same as in other languages:

```
var x = 2;
x++; // x = x + 1 (3)
x--; // x = x - 1 (2)
```

You can also use the += operator for strings (but using any of the other assignment operators with strings will return NaN):

```
var x = 'Hello ';
x += 'world!'; // Hello world!
```

Functions

There are two main ways of defining a function in JavaScript: the function declaration and the function expression. For example:

```
// Function declaration
function greet(name) {
        console.log('Hello ' + name + '!');
}

// Function expression (anonymous function)
var greet2 = function (name) {
        console.log('Hello ' + name + '!');
};
```

Function expressions can either be named or anonymous. They have a fairly similar syntax, but the named function has a .name property, which can be used for backtracing, usually by the browser:

```
// Anonymous function expression
var greet3 = function (name) {
        // ...
};
console.log(greet3.name); // blank string

// Named function expression
```

```
var greet4 = function greet (name) {
    // ...
};
console.log(greet4.name); // greet
```

It is worth noting that the `.name` property is not actually part of the JavaScript specification, and attempting to access it will result in an error in Internet Explorer—if you want global support for your code, you shouldn't use this property.

A function declaration and a function expression look and behave in very similar ways, but the former is *hoisted*, meaning that it appears at the top of the scope (the function or file) so that it can be called before it is actually defined. Function expressions also look much better as arguments for other functions (we'll get to that in a bit).

We use the same syntax to call each type of function:

```
greet('Alien'); // Hello Alien!
greet2('World'); // Hello World!
```

Hoisting Example

As foo is a function declaration, it is *hoisted*, meaning that it goes at the beginning of the scope—either the top of the page (in this case) or the top of the function. This means that it is available before it is defined from the top of the scope, so typeof foo returns function. As bar is only a function expression, it isn't available until after it has been defined, so typeof bar returns undefined:

```
console.log(typeof foo); // function
console.log(typeof bar); // undefined

function foo() {}
var bar = function () {};
```

This behavior can have some pretty weird side effects. For example:

```
// Example one
function test() {
    return 'one';
}

console.log(test()); // two

function test() {
    return 'two';
}


// Example two
if (true) {
    function test2() {
```

```
            return 'one';
        }
    } else {
        function test2() {
            return 'two';
        }
    }

    console.log(test2()); // two
```

We can work around both of these example scenarios fairly easily by using a function expression.

Variable declarations are also hoisted, but that affects you as a developer far less than function hoisting does (which is why it was mentioned here, not under the string section). Only the declaration itself is hoisted; the actual assignment is not. The only real effect this has is that if you define a variable as a later point in the function, you cannot access the variable from a parent scope:

```
var a = 'foo';

var b = function () {
        console.log(a); // undefined
        var a = 'bar';
};
b();
```

As it is common practice to put all variable function declarations at the top of the function (and it is definitely something that I would encourage you to make a habit of), this isn't a massive issue.

Functions as Arguments

Functions can also be sent as arguments to functions, like this:

```
function call(func, data) {
        func(data);
}

call(function (a) {
        console.log(a);
}, 'Test');
```

This function, while slightly more complicated than any of the previous code examples in this book, is actually pretty simple. First, we define a function that simply calls the function sent to it (in this case, the anonymous function), and then we call it. This sort of syntax is used a lot in jQuery, usually for callbacks:

```
$('a.bounce').click(function () {
        // Do something with the element
});
```

This code, when jQuery detects that a.bounce has been clicked, calls the anonymous function.

Returning a Value

We can also return a value from a function:

```
function product(a, b) {
        return a * b;
}

console.log(product(2, 4)); // 8
console.log(product(10, 0)); // 0
```

If we do not specify a return value, undefined is returned:

```
function blank() {
        // no return statement
}

console.log(blank()); // undefined
```

Objects

An object is a way of storing a collection of indexed data. Again, it is easiest to explain with an example:

```
var your_obj = {
        foo: 'bar',
        otherIndex: 2 + 2
};

console.log(your_obj.foo); // bar
console.log(your_obj.otherIndex); // 4
```

The object is defined using curly braces, and allows data to be stored by keys (known as *properties*). This notation is known as the *object literal notation*. We can access and modify objects using the dot operator, and delete items using the delete keyword:

```
your_obj.foo = 'test';
console.log(your_obj.foo); // test

delete your_obj.foo;
console.log(your_obj.foo); // undefined
```

You can store any type of data in an object, including other objects.

```
var obj = {
        foo: {
                foo: 'bar'
```

```
    }
};

console.log(obj.foo.foo); // bar
```

Here is where it starts to get a little more complicated, though. Almost everything is an object in JavaScript (which is why we can use functions as arguments). For example, we can treat a function like an object, setting and accessing properties and methods:

```
var foo = function () {};
foo.hello = 'world';
console.log(foo); // function () {}
console.log(foo.hello); // world

console.log(foo.length); // 0
```

As demonstrated here, objects have built-in properties that they inherit from the object from which they were created (in this case, the Function object). 'string'.length would return the length of the string, which in this case is 6, and (function(){}).length would return the number of arguments it accepts, which in this case is 0. Objects also have built-in methods:

```
console.log('string'.toUpperCase()); // STRING
```

MDN (*http://mzl.la/RKxal6*) (Mozilla Developer Network) has some extremely good JavaScript references. It has a list of all the string methods here (*http://mzl.la/ 11nBlYi*), where you can find all the methods for the other objects, like Arrays and Objects.

Just as functions can be treated as objects, we can have variables that are accessible as both an object and a function. This is how jQuery's $ variable works. We can simulate the behavior using the following code:

```
function $(selector) {
        return document.querySelectorAll(selector);
}

// Loops through elements
$.each = function (array, cb) {
        for (var i = 0; i < array.length; i++) {
                cb.call(i, array[i], array);
        }
}

var paragraphs = $('p'); // returns all paragraphs
$.each(paragraphs, function (index, paragraph) {
        // ...
});
```

This isn't exactly how jQuery works (the function returns a real NodeList instead of a jQuery node list, which is covered in Chapter 3), but the principle is the same.

Finding the Type of a Variable

You can use the `typeof` operator to find out what type of data a variable contains. This has a lot of practical applications, such as checking whether variables are the correct type (e.g., checking whether the input in a string function is in fact a string) or checking whether a variable is defined:

```
var str = '';
console.log(typeof str); // string
console.log(typeof 4); // number
console.log(typeof {}); // object
```

The five types are `string`, `number`, `object`, `function`, and `boolean`. It can also return `undefined`, which means that the variable hasn't been defined.

Sometimes the operator can return some weird things:

```
console.log(typeof null); // object
console.log(typeof NaN); // number
```

A variable that is `null` doesn't contain anything; it's sort of a halfway point between `undefined` and an empty string. `NaN` means "Not a Number," and is returned when you try to do impossible mathematical operations such as `"a" / 2`.

To work around these, you can use the following:

```
var null_var = null;
console.log(null_var === null); // true
console.log(isNaN(NaN)); // true
```

We'll learn more about the `===` operator in "Comparison Operators" (page 83); it just means "equal to."

Arrays

Arrays are similar to objects, but their contents are accessed differently and they do not have properties like objects, just numeric values known as *indexes*:

```
var foo = ['one', 'two', 'three'];

console.log(foo[0]); // one
console.log(foo[2]); // three
```

As with pretty much everything in computing, lists are indexed from the number 0.

Arrays have a number of built-in methods that you can use to modify the array. To add new items to arrays, you can use the `.push` method:

```
var foo = ['one', 'two'];
foo.push('three');

console.log(foo[0]); // one
console.log(foo[2]); // three
```

To delete an item from the array, you can use the .splice method. In addition to deleting items, .splice also allows you to add new items to the middle of the array:

```
var foo = ['one', 'junk', 'more junk', 'three'];
foo.splice(1, 2, 'two');

console.log(foo[0]); // one
console.log(foo[2]); // three
```

This deletes two items from the item with index 1 (junk) and replaces them with two. The third argument is optional, so you can just delete items without replacing them, too:

```
var foo = ['one', 'two', 'junk', 'three'];
foo.splice(2, 1);

console.log(foo[0]); // one
console.log(foo[2]); // three
```

Consult MDN (*http://mzl.la/Wyiani*) to see a full list of the array methods available.

Detecting an Array

As typeof [] returns "object", we cannot use it to detect an array. Instead, we can use the instanceof operator or the Array.isArray function:

```
console.log([] instanceof Array); // true
console.log(Array.isArray([])); // true
```

The instanceof operator isn't too reliable, as it can be tricked into returning the wrong answer. The best way of detecting an array is definitely to use the Array.isArray function. However, it is relatively new (it was introduced in JavaScript 1.8.5), and thus isn't supported in Internet Explorer 7 and lower. There are two ways around this. The first is to use jQuery's jQuery.isArray function:

```
console.log($.isArray([])); // true
console.log($.isArray({})); // false
```

The second workaround is to create the Array.isArray function if it doesn't exist. The following snippet of code is from MDN:

```
if(!Array.isArray) {
  Array.isArray = function (vArg) {
    return Object.prototype.toString.call(vArg) === "[object Array]";
  };
}
```

This can be called the same way `Array.isArray` is called.

Looping

Loops are found in nearly every modern computing language, and are a very powerful feature. Their name is fairly descriptive: loops allow you to repeat the same block of code. This is good for, say, looping through arrays of objects.

The for Loop

The first loop we'll look at is the `for` loop. It is a common way of looping through arrays:

```
var foo = ['one', 'two', 'three'];
for (var i = 0; i < foo.length; i++) {
        console.log(foo[i]);
}
```

This results in the three elements being individually logged to the console. The loop is, again, quite simple: `var i = 0` defines `i` as 0; `i < foo.length` returns `false` when `i` is not less than `foo.length`, stopping the loop; and `i++` is the equivalent of `i = i + 1`, as explained in "Numbers" (page 71).

The first statement, `var i = 0`, is run once, before the first iteration. The third statement, `i++`, is run every single time. The second statement is the conditional that tells the loop when to stop looping. If the result of the second statement is either `false` or `0`, then the loop stops running (`null`, `undefined`, or a blank string won't stop the loop).

In modern browsers, there is a more elegant solution available for looping through arrays. If you have used a language such as PHP, you will have used the `foreach` loop before. This was introduced in JavaScript recently, so doesn't have support in all browsers, but it is a lot cleaner (although slightly different from implementations in other languages). The following code outputs exactly the same as the previous code example:

```
var foo = ['one', 'two', 'three'];
foo.forEach(function (value, index) {
        console.log(value);
});
```

For support in older browsers, it is worth either using a `for` loop or a loop from a library. (MDN also has a workaround for this to add `.forEach` support in older browsers; check out the `.foreach` page (*http://mzl.la/XX4VDg*).) Nearly all libraries have functions like this, and jQuery is no exception. The `jQuery.each` function behaves in a very similar manner to the `foreach` loop:

```
var foo = ['one', 'two', 'three'];
$.each(foo, function (index, value) {
        console.log(value);
});
```

That will output the same as both the previous loop examples.

There is another method that is similar to `Array.forEach`: `Array.map`. It cycles through the array, running the given function on each element, and creating a new array from the return values, which is then returned, leaving the original array intact. For example, the following code will take an array of numbers and return an array of those numbers squared:

```
var numbers = [1, 2, 3, 5, 10];

var newNumbers = numbers.map(function (number) {
        return Math.pow(number, 2);
});

console.log(newNumbers); // [1, 4, 9, 25, 100]
```

Similarly to `Array.forEach`, jQuery provides a function so that you can use this behavior in browsers that don't support `map` natively. As you can see, it is fairly easy to use:

```
var numbers = [1, 2, 3, 5, 10];

var newNumbers = $.map(numbers, function (number) {
        return Math.pow(number, 2);
});

console.log(newNumbers); // [1, 4, 9, 25, 100]
```

It behaves exactly the same, and leaves the original array intact.

For a `map` function that would work in every browser without jQuery, you can use a `for` loop:

```
var numbers = [1, 2, 3, 5, 10],
        newNumbers = [];

for (var i = 0; i < numbers.length; i++) {
        newNumbers.push(Math.pow(number, 2));
}

console.log(newNumbers); // [1, 4, 9, 25, 100]
```

The while Loop

The `while` loop executes the contained code while a given conditional is `true`:

```
var i = 0;
while (i < 100) {
        console.log(i);
        i++;
}
```

This outputs the numbers 0 to 99. The reason it wouldn't output 100 is that i is incremented after it is logged to the console, meaning that when it hits 100, i < 100 will return false and the loop will be stopped.

Developers use a while loop fairly often to count down instead of using a for loop to count up. If order doesn't matter (or you need to go backward), cycling through backward can be a lot more efficient, as there is only one statement per iteration (i--), as opposed to two with a for loop (i <= 100 and i++). The following code will output the numbers 99 to 0 inclusive:

```
var i = 100;
while (i--) {
        console.log(i);
}
```

The do-while Loop

The do-while loop is similar to the while loop, but the conditional is after the code block, which changes the behavior slightly and ensures that the loop will always be run once:

```
var i = 0;
do {
        i++;
} while (false);
console.log(i); // 1
```

With loops such as in the preceding subsection's while loop example, do-while will behave exactly the same. The following code will output the numbers 0 to 99:

```
var i = 0;
do {
        console.log(i);
        i++;
} while (i < 100);
```

The break and continue Statements

You can use break to break out of any loop, and you can use continue to stop executing the code block and move to the next iteration.

The following code sample is an example of the break statement. It is similar to the previous code sample, but will only output the numbers 0 to 50, as when i++ increases i to 51, i > 50 will return true and break will be called, stopping the loop:

```
var i = 0;
while (i < 100) {
        console.log(i);
        i++;
        if (i > 50) {
                break;
        }
}
```

The break statement can be useful if the conditional to stop a loop is too big; you can make the loop infinite using while (true), and then have the break statement in an if statement—or have a couple of if statements. You should be careful while doing this, though, as messing up the conditional in the if statement would cause a real infinite loop.

The following example demonstrates the continue statement. It expands on the previous example, but the continue before the if statement will ensure that the break statement will never run; the numbers 0 to 99 will be logged:

```
var i = 0;
while (i < 100) {
        console.log(i);
        i++;
        continue;
        if (i > 50) {
                break;
        }
}
```

for..in statements

for..in statements are used to loop through an object:

```
var foo = {
        one: 1,
        two: 2
};

for (var prop in foo) {
        console.log(prop + ': ' + foo[prop]);
}
```

This outputs one: 1 and then two: 2. As you can see, it assigned prop to be the property, not the value itself, so the value had to be retrieved via foo[prop].

Conditional Statements

The if Statement

The if statement executes some code if a given conditional is true:

```
if (true) {
        // Execute code
}
if (false) {
        // Code here won't be executed
}
```

In addition to the simple if statement, you can also use else if and else:

```
if (i < 10) {
        // i is less than ten
} else if (i < 15) {
        // i is less than 15 and more than or equal to ten
} else {
        // i is more than or equal to 15
}
```

Comparison Operators

As seen in the for and while loops, it is possible to use < to determine whether one number is smaller than another number. There are also a number of other comparison operators listed in Table A-1.

Table A-1. Comparison operators (examples return true)

Operator	Description	Example
==	The two inputs are equal.	4 == "4"
===	The two inputs are the same.	'a' === 'a'
!=	The two inputs are not equal.	7 != 4
!==	The two inputs are not the same.	4 !== "4"
<	The first input is less than the second input.	2 < 6
>	The first input is greater than the second.	"f" > "c"
<=	The first input is less than or equal to the second.	2 <= 2
>=	The first input is greater than or equal to the second.	5 >= 3

The difference between == and === is that === checks whether the inputs are the same type, while == does not. For example, 0 == false and '0' == 0 would return true, while 0 === false and '0' === 0 would not.

Objects (including arrays and functions), when compared via == and ===, act slightly differently than strings and numbers; these operations will return `true` if the objects are the same, but `false` if they aren't:

```
var ary = [], obj = {};
console.log(ary == []); // false
console.log(ary === []); // false
console.log(ary == ary); // true
console.log(obj === obj); // true
```

If you want to compare two objects or arrays, you must loop through them and compare the contents. Comparing objects and arrays can be useful in testing libraries (in fact, it is often essential).

 When comparing two different objects, check the lengths before looping through them; if they're not the same length, then you know they're not the same and so there is no need to loop through them.

Logical Operators

Logical operators are used to group multiple conditional statements together; see Table A-2.

Table A-2. Logical operators (examples return true)

Operator	Description	Example
&&	"And": both are true.	`true && true`
||	"Or": one is true.	`false || true`
!	Negates the value given to it.	`!false`

For example:

```
if (age < 18 || age > 25) {
        // age is either less than 18 OR above 25
}

if (age > 18 && gender === 'male') {
        // age is greater than 18 AND gender is male
}

if (!age) {
        // age is falsy
}
```

You can use two negation logical operators to cast a variable to Boolean (true or false):

```
console.log(!!''); // false
console.log(!!7); // true
```

In an if statement, you don't need to cast the variable to Boolean.

Falsy values

In the last comment in the preceding code example, I referred to a variable as *falsy*. A falsy variable is one where it evaluates to false; it is either false, undefined, '', 0, or null. Everything else is *truthy*. In the aforementioned example, it was probably either 0 or '' (assuming that we're accepting input from a form).

In the context of an if statement, statements that return falsy will cause the block to not be evaluated:

```
if (false) {
        // will not be run
}
if (undefined) {
        // will not be run
}
if ('' || 0 || null) {
        // will not be run
}
```

Any other value (a truthy value) will cause the block to be evaluated:

```
if ([]) {
        // will be run
}
if ('Hello world!') {
        // will be run
}
if (-1) {
        // will be run
}
```

The switch Statement

The switch statement executes a block of code specified by a value:

```
var foo = 'bar';
switch (foo) {
        case 'a':
                console.log('This will not be logged');
                break;

        case 'bar':
```

```
            console.log('This will be logged');
            break;

    case 'foo':
            console.log('This will not be logged');
            break;
}
```

The statement will take the value given to it (in this case, bar) and run the code from the given case statement until it hits a break statement or the closing parenthesis. In the preceding code, the switch statement will run the code from case 'bar': to the break on the line below the console.log, meaning that it will be the only console.log called.

We can also have multiple case statements:

```
var foo = 'bar';
switch (foo) {
        case 'a':
                console.log('Will not be logged');
                break;

        case 'bar':
        case 'foo':
                console.log('Will be logged');
                break;
}
```

Then, while Will be logged will be logged if foo is equal to bar, it will also be logged if foo is equal to foo.

There is one more statement: the default statement. If no cases match the variable, then the default statement will be called:

```
switch (foo) {
        case 'bar':
                console.log('Will be called if the foo variable equals bar');
                break;

        default:
                console.log('Will be called if foo equals anything else');
                break;
}
```

We'll use a new object, Date, for a more complicated example of a switch statement:

```
switch (new Date().getDay()) {
        case 5:
                console.log('Friday!');
                break;

        case 6:
        case 0:
```

```
            console.log('Weekend!');
            break;

    default:
            console.log('Weekday :-(');
            break;
    }
```

The `Date` object is a native JavaScript object for performing date and time functions. `new Date()` creates a new instance of the `Date` object with the current date and time, and the `.getDay()` method returns the day of the week where 0 is Sunday and 6 is a Saturday.

If we omit the `break` statement, the code will "fall through," and both the current case and the next will be executed:

```
switch (new Date().getDay()) {
    case 0:
    case 6:
            console.log('The week has passed');

    case 5:
            console.log('Thursday has passed');

    case 4:
            console.log('Wednesday has passed');

    case 3:
            console.log('Tuesday has passed');

    case 2:
            console.log('Monday has passed');
    }
```

On Wednesday, both "Tuesday has passed" and "Monday has passed" will be logged, and on the weekend everything will be logged. On Monday, nothing will be logged.

This technique is often considered fairly bad practice—it can sometimes make debugging difficult, and if you accidentally miss a `break` statement, it will make your code behave strangely and will be difficult to catch. I would say that it's fine to use in moderation, but be very careful.

If you've only got one bit of code per case, then it can often be a lot easier (and certainly a lot cleaner and easier to debug) to just use an object. The following three code samples will do exactly the same thing:

```
// Using a switch statement:

switch (randLetter()) {
    case 'A':
            console.log('The function returned A');
```

```javascript
                break;

        case 'E':
                console.log('This time, the function returned E');
                break;

        case 'I':
                console.log('I!');
                break;

        case 'O':
                console.log('Oh, the function returned "O"');
                break;

        case 'U':
                console.log('You? Ewe? Yew?');
                break;

        default:
                console.log('The function returned an inferior letter');
                break;
}

// Using an object
var letters = {
        A: function () {
                console.log('The function returned A');
        },
        E: function () {
                console.log('This time, the function returned E');
        },
        I: function () {
                console.log('I!');
        },
        O: function () {
                console.log('Oh, the function returned "O"');
        },
        U: function () {
                console.log('You? Ewe? Yew?');
        },
        default: function () {
                console.log('The function returned an inferior letter');
        }
};

var letter = randLetter();
if (letters[letter]) {
        letters[letter].call();
} else {
        letters.default();
}
```

```
// Or even:
var letters = {
        A: 'The function returned A',
        E: 'This time, the function returned E',
        I: 'I!',
        O: 'Oh, the function returned "O"',
        U: 'You? Ewe? Yew?',
        default: 'The function returned an inferior letter'
};

console.log(letters[randLetter()] || letters.default);
```

Delays

There are two functions built into JavaScript that allow you to implement a delay into your code. The first, setTimeout, calls the given function after a specified time interval (specified in milliseconds, a thousandth of a second). The following code waits one second and then logs "Hello world!" to the console:

```
setTimeout(function () {
        console.log('Hello world!');
}, 1000);
```

As JavaScript is an asynchronous language, this would not stop the code below from running. The following code would log one to the console after 500 ms, and then two 500 ms after that. To have one logged 500 ms after two was logged, we would either have to adjust the time on the second timeout to be 1,500 ms, or we would have to put it in the anonymous function that is being called by the first setTimeout:

```
setTimeout(function () {
        console.log('two');
}, 1000);

setTimeout(function () {
        console.log('one');
}, 500);
```

The second function that allows you to work with delays is setInterval, which calls the given function every *x* milliseconds, instead of just once like setTimeout does. The code function logs "Hello world!" to the console every two seconds:

```
setInterval(function () {
        console.log('Hello world!');
}, 2000);
```

When you call either setTimeout or setInterval, it returns a number that can then be passed to clearTimeout or clearInterval to stop the timeout or interval from running:

```
var id = setInterval(function () {
        console.log('Hello world1');
}, 500);

setTimeout(function () {
        clearInterval(id);
}, 5050);
```

That code would log "Hello world!" to the console twice a second for five seconds, at which point it would stop. The 5,050 is to ensure that it happens 10 times; if it were 5,000, it would only happen nine times, and it could be misunderstood if 5,500 were used. clearTimeout works the same way; setTimeout returns an ID that can then be passed to clearTimeout to cancel the running of the timeout. Obviously, if the timeout has already run, clearing it won't do anything.

Regular Expressions

Regular expressions, commonly known as "regex" or "RegExp," are a very powerful tool used to parse data. To people who haven't met them before, regular expressions can seem to have a somewhat confusing syntax, but as you learn and get used to them, they become clearer and easier to write. As regular expressions aren't exclusive to JavaScript—the syntax most commonly used is from Perl—I won't explain regular expressions themselves, just how to use them in JavaScript. To find out more about regular expressions generally, read *Mastering Regular Expressions* (*http://oreil.ly/ Mastering_RegEx*) by Jeffrey E. F. Friedl.

There are two ways to create a regular expression in JavaScript. The first is the preferred way, but if you want to accept user input into the regular expression, then you have to use the second:

```
var regex = /(?:foo)+/g;
var regex2 = new RegExp('^' + username + ': (.+)$', 'i');
```

The first method utilizes the RegExp literal, while the second just creates a new instance of the RegExp object. Both methods have the same end result, but the first is more readable and slightly more efficient; I have explained why in greater detail in Chapter 5.

For the regex variable, (?:foo)+ is the regular expression itself, and g is the modifier. For the regex2 variable, '^' + username + ': (.+)$' generates the regular expression, and the i modifier is used.

There are two main methods used to execute regular expressions, .exec and .test. Both are methods of the regular expression and accept a string input:

```
var regex = /^hello/ig; // tests whether string begins with "hello"
regex.test('Hello world!'); // true
regex.exec('Hello world!'); // ["hello"]
regex.test('Foo bar'); // false
regex.exec('Foo bar'); // null
```

.test returns a Boolean value denoting whether the regex matches the string, while .exec returns the array. Any capturing groups return their contents as part of the returned array (they wouldn't affect the output of .test, though):

```
var regex = /^hello ([^ ]+)!$/i;
regex.exec('Hello world!'); // ["Hello world!", "world"]
```

Regular Expressions in String Functions

Some string functions also accept regular expressions as arguments:

```
"abcdefg".split(/[c|e]/g); // ["ab", "d", "fg"]
"abcdefg".search(/[c|e]/g); // 2
"abcdefg".match(/[c|e]/g); // ["c", "e"]
"abcdefg".replace(/(c|e)/g, 'x'); // abxdxfg
```

For .match and .replace, remember to use the global modifier. If you don't, only the first instance will be matched and the output will be very different, as demonstrated in the following example. You don't need to use the global modifier for .split and .search, as .split seems to ignore it and .search only returns the index of the first instance anyway:

```
"abcdefg".split(/[c|e]/); // ["ab", "d", "fg"]
"abcdefg".search(/[c|e]/); // 2
"abcdefg".match(/[c|e]/); // ["c"]
"abcdefg".replace(/(c|e)/, 'x'); // abxdefg
```

Error Handling

The JavaScript way of handling errors is fairly similar to how errors work in other languages. We can throw errors using a throw statement:

```
throw new Error('This is an error');
```

This will display the error in the console, as you can see in Figure A-3.

Figure A-3. Throwing an error

All runtime errors are thrown like this as well. You can catch and handle errors using a try-catch statement, like in other languages:

```
try {
        throw new Error('Test');
} catch (e) {
        console.log(e);
}
```

This will just result in your Error object being logged to the console. Executing a throw statement stops the execution of code in the current block, so it is important to catch errors or your application could die silently, leaving the user wondering what is happening. The error objects created have two properties, name and message. name is the name property from the constructor function, and could be Error, one of the other built-in constructors such as TypeError or ReferenceError, or a custom constructor, which I will cover in a bit. message is just the string that was passed to the constructor, which was 'Test' in the previous example.

Besides the Error object, JavaScript has six other error constructors built in, as listed in Table A-3.

Table A-3. Error constructors

Constructor	Description
EvalError	Thrown when you use eval improperly.
RangeError	Thrown when you pass a number to a function that is outside the allowed range—for example, if you try to create an array of length -1.
ReferenceError	Thrown when you try to reference a variable that does not exist.
SyntaxError	Thrown when you pass invalid code to eval.
TypeError	Thrown when a variable or argument is of the wrong type—for example, if you try to access a property of an undefined variable.
URIError	Thrown when you give the encodeURI or decodeURI functions invalid arguments.

It is also possible to create your own error types using the `Error` object:

```
function CustomError(message) {
        this.name = 'CustomError';
        this.message = message;
}

CustomError.prototype = new Error();
CustomError.prototype.constructor = CustomError;

throw new CustomError('This is a custom error');
```

That will usually result in something like `"CustomError: This is a custom error"` being displayed in the console, an example of which you can see in Figure A-4.

Figure A-4. Throwing a custom error

Summary

In this chapter, you learned the fundamentals of JavaScript:

- You create strings using quotes (`"string"` and `'string'`) and concatenate them using the + operator.
- You learned how to work with numbers—specifically, arithmetic operations using `*`, `/`, `+`, and `-`, and the assignment operator shortcuts such as += and /=.
- Functions allow you to reuse code. There are three different types:
  — Anonymous function expressions: `var func = function () {};`.
  — Named function expressions: `var func = function func () {};`.
  — Function declarations: `function func() {}`.
- You can return values using `return`.
- You can call functions using the following syntax: `greet('World')`.

- You can create objects (collections of indexed data) using the object literals (`var obj = {};`), and you can access and modify properties using the dot operator. Delete object properties using the `delete` keyword.
- Boolean data is the simplest form of data: `true` or `false`.
- You can retrieve the type of a variable using `typeof`: `typeof {} === 'object'`.

Comment code using either single-line comments:

```
// This is a single line comment
```

or multiline comments:

```
/* This can span multiple lines */
```

Arrays can be used to store nonindexed lists of information. You can create these using the array literal, `var ary = ['one', 'two']`, and you can access and modify items using indexes: `ary[0] === 'one'`. You can detect arrays using `instanceof` and `Array.isArray()`, but not `typeof` because it returns `'object'`.

There are three main loops. The first, the `for` loop, can loop through arrays and objects like this:

```
// Cycle through arrays
for (var i = 0; i < ary.length; i++) {
        // ...
}

for (var prop in obj) {
        // ...
}
```

The `while` loop is used to loop while a certain condition is true, and the `do-while` loop is used in a very similar way, but will always run the given code at least once:

```
while (i < 27) {
        // ...
}

do {
        // ...
} while (i < 27);
```

Newer browsers support a `forEach` method on `Array` objects, which can be used like this:

```
['one', 'two'].forEach(function (value, index) {
        console.log(value);
});
```

Conditionals (e.g., `myVar > 10`) can be used to control the flow of the script via `if`, `if-else`, and `else` statements. There are many different conditionals available, such as `==`, `!==`, `<=`, and `>`. We can use logical operators to group the conditionals together. `&&` will return `true` if both conditionals are true, and `||` will return `true` if one is true. Finally, we can use the negation operator (`!`) to negate a value.

`setTimeout` and `setInterval` allow you to put delays in your code, and run code at every specified time interval:

```
setTimeout(function () {
        // ...
}, 1000);
```

We can define regular expressions using either the `RegExp` object, which accepts two arguments—`new RegExp('[a-z]+', 'g')`—or the regular expression literal —`/[a-z]+/g`. We can use regexes with their `.exec` and `.test` methods, and there are also several string functions that accept regex arguments.

We can throw errors using the `throw` statement: `throw new Error('This is an ex ample error')`, and catch them again by using a `try-catch` statement. In addition to the `Error` object, there are six built-in error objects—including `SyntaxError` and `TypeError`—and you can also create your own custom error objects.

JavaScript Resources

There are many resources, both applications and websites, that you can use to aid your JavaScript development.

A Good IDE

Your editor is your most useful tool when coding. I prefer IDEs (integrated development environments) to normal text editors, as they usually include additional tools such as debugging tools, file and database management, and sometimes support for version control software. You can see an example of an IDE (in this case, JetBrains PhpStorm, my IDE of preference) in Figure B-1. When I'm coding, I have only my IDE, a browser (usually Chrome), a terminal, and a music player open; my IDE includes a regex toolkit that can test my regular expressions for me, a powerful debugger (although it doesn't actually support JavaScript, hence my use of Chrome), and an HTTP inspector for when Chrome isn't enough.

Some IDEs may cost a lot—mine did—but I have found that in the majority of cases, the best ones are the more expensive ones. A free or cheap IDE may claim to have tons of features that a more expensive rival may not, but it may be difficult to use, poorly researched, and buggy. I would recommend trying more than one IDE before deciding which to use. Most of the paid ones have free trials available, so make sure to give them a try.

GitHub

GitHub (*https://github.com/*) is a huge website that hosts Git repositories. It offers free hosting to open source projects, and paid accounts are also available for people who want to hide their repositories from the public. But it isn't just that—it also adds features to Git that make developing much easier. It allows you to view the code from

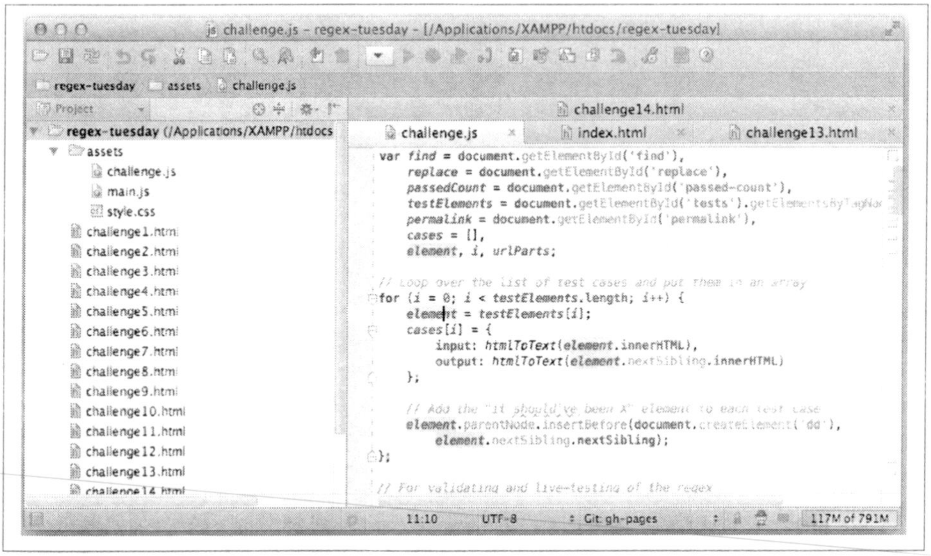

Figure B-1. JetBrains PhpStorm

the website, which can be very useful for viewing other people's projects, and it also allows you to view the commit history of a project. In addition, instead of commits being tagged with a name and an email address, they are tagged with the GitHub account of the committer, so you can view everything that person has contributed, what projects she has contributed to, and various other statistics.

GitHub also provides other functions for Git repositories, such as an issue tracker for each repository, a wiki, and a static website. It also shows some helpful graphs, such as impact (which developers have contributed what), traffic, clones, and fork information.

JSHint

JSHint (*http://jshint.com/*) is a syntax checker that checks your code for bad practices and warns you about them. It is based on JSLint, which is a similar tool written by Douglas Crockford. However, some people (including me) find JSLint far too strict about some things, and so JSHint was written. You can see a screenshot of JSHint in action—in this case, checking for problems in the functions from Chapter 1—in Figure B-2.

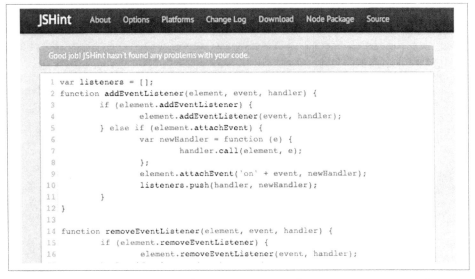

Figure B-2. JSHint testing the addEventListener and removeEventListener functions from Chapter 1

JSPerf

JSPerf (*http://jsperf.com/*) is a great website for testing the performance of JavaScript samples (Figure B-3 shows it in action). You can enter multiple code samples, and it will test them all to see which performs the most iterations per second, and is fastest. It then saves the results and displays them in a graph compared to all the other browsers that have performed that test, making it very easy to compare the code across multiple browsers.

As an example, let's test whether it's worth caching the result of a call to jQuery if it's going to be called multiple times. You could add the following two test cases:

```
// First test case
$('#foo');
$('#foo');
$('#foo');

// Second test case
var foo = $('#foo');
foo;
foo;
foo;
```

Obviously, the second test case will be three times faster than the first test case; they contain basically exactly the same code, but the first contains it three times. But is it worth caching? Does it save only a few nanoseconds per iteration? If so, it probably isn't worth worrying about.

Test runner		
Done. Ready to run again.		Run again
Testing in Chrome 18.0.1025.168 on Mac OS X 10.8.0		
Test		**Ops/sec**
getElementById	`document.getElementById('foo');`	15,361,130 ±0.60% fastest
jQuery	`$('#foo');`	1,046,876 ±1.58% 93% slower

Figure B-3. Test case from Chapter 3

Mozilla Developer Network

The Mozilla Developer Network (MDN) contains a huge array of resources and documentation for frontend developers. Searching the website, you can find articles, tutorials, links to useful tools, and documentation on pretty much every JavaScript function, object, and method.

You can find it at *https://developer.mozilla.org/en-US/*.

Pastebins

A pastebin is a place to dump code to share with others. For example, if you're stuck with a piece of code or you just want to show off how awesome something you wrote is, then you can paste it into the pastebin and it will give you a link to share with other people. Pastebins usually have built-in syntax highlighters that it will apply to your code. The most commonly used pastebin is Pastebin.com (*http://pastebin.com/*), which at the time of writing boasts over 17 million pastes. However, its syntax highlighter for JavaScript isn't great and can be difficult to read. For this reason, I usually use another pastebin.

Gist

Gist (*https://gist.github.com/*) is GitHub's pastebin. It has excellent syntax highlighting for JavaScript, and allows you to fork and clone pastes and see the difference between different revisions of pastes. It isn't as complicated as I make it sound, and is extremely powerful.

JSFiddle

Something similar to a pastebin (but I wouldn't classify it as a pastebin) is JSFiddle (*http://jsfiddle.net/*). It allows you to paste your HTML, JavaScript, and CSS in, and it will then run it for you. You can then save it and send the link to other people, and they can see and edit your page. This is useful for the same reason that normal pastebins are useful, except with the added functionality; as well as fixing your code, it allows people to test their edits and debug your existing code. You can see a screenshot of me editing some code from Chapter 1 in Figure B-4.

Figure B-4. Fiddle for some code from Chapter 2: View here (http://jsfiddle.net/Hm9k4/)

Version Control Software

Version control software (sometimes known as *revision software*) is a way of saving "snapshots" of your code. I'll explain this in terms of Git, as it is the version control system I use on a regular basis and the only one I am familiar enough with to write about. Other version control systems include SVN and Mercurial.

When you make a change in your code, you can *commit* the changes. This means that for every change (usually a feature or bug fix), there is a commit. At any point you can modify the changes made in a commit or remove a previous commit, which means that you can undo changes without having to do it manually. You can also, if you break something, revert to the last commit without having to manually undo every change that you have made; this can prove extremely useful.

Version control systems can also be useful for collaborating with other developers on the same piece of code. You can *branch* the code (i.e., create a copy of the code), do your work, commit the changes, and merge the changes back into the master branch. Multiple branches can be created, and Git is especially good at merging conflicting changes (for example, from multiple developers working simultaneously on the same file). Unless the developers have changed the same line, no manual intervention is required.

Version control systems also include many other features, and can often significantly speed up development time.

About the Author

Callum Macrae is a professional JavaScript developer based in the UK. He regularly contributes JavaScript-related patches to open source projects, including phpBB and jQuery++. When not coding or writing, he spends most of his time drumming or cycling.

Colophon

The animal on the cover of *Learning from jQuery* is an Asian green broadbill (*Calyptomena viridis*). It is distinct from the African green broadbill (*Pseudocalyptomena graueri*), also known as the Grauer's broadbill. Despite Walter Rothschild christening the Grauer's broadbill *pseudocalyptomena*, or "false" Calyptomena, modern science has discovered that this bird is, in fact, related to the Asian green broadbill. Thus, both this bird and its cousin are true broadbill birds.

The Asian green broadbill is a small bird, averaging 15 cm in length. It has brilliant green and blue plumage, with black bars on its wings and a puff of feathers just above its beak. The broadbill is so named for its broad beak, although the beak itself is weak because this species primarily feeds on figs.

The broadbill inhabits evergreen trees in Malaysian and Indonesian forests, and is still fairly common, despite increasing habitat loss. This bird makes its nest out of lichen and spider webs, which camouflages the nests to look like arboreal litter.

The cover image is from *Johnson's Natural History*. The cover font is Adobe ITC Garamond. The text font is Adobe Minion Pro; the heading font is Adobe Myriad Condensed; and the code font is Dalton Maag's Ubuntu Mono.

Have it your way.

O'Reilly eBooks

- Lifetime access to the book when you buy through oreilly.com
- Provided in up to four DRM-free file formats, for use on the devices of your choice: PDF, .epub, Kindle-compatible .mobi, and Android .apk
- Fully searchable, with copy-and-paste and print functionality
- Alerts when files are updated with corrections and additions

oreilly.com/ebooks/

Safari Books Online

- Access the contents and quickly search over 7000 books on technology, business, and certification guides
- Learn from expert video tutorials, and explore thousands of hours of video on technology and design topics
- Download whole books or chapters in PDF format, at no extra cost, to print or read on the go
- Get early access to books as they're being written
- Interact directly with authors of upcoming books
- Save up to 35% on O'Reilly print books

See the complete Safari Library at safari.oreilly.com

O'REILLY®

Get even more for your money.

Join the O'Reilly Community, and register the O'Reilly books you own. It's free, and you'll get:

- $4.99 ebook upgrade offer
- 40% upgrade offer on O'Reilly print books
- Membership discounts on books and events
- Free lifetime updates to ebooks and videos
- Multiple ebook formats, DRM FREE
- Participation in the O'Reilly community
- Newsletters
- Account management
- 100% Satisfaction Guarantee

Signing up is easy:

1. **Go to: oreilly.com/go/register**
2. **Create an O'Reilly login.**
3. **Provide your address.**
4. **Register your books.**

Note: English-language books only

To order books online:
oreilly.com/store

For questions about products or an order:
orders@oreilly.com

To sign up to get topic-specific email announcements and/or news about upcoming books, conferences, special offers, and new technologies:
elists@oreilly.com

For technical questions about book content:
booktech@oreilly.com

To submit new book proposals to our editors:
proposals@oreilly.com

O'Reilly books are available in multiple DRM-free ebook formats. For more information:
oreilly.com/ebooks

Spreading the knowledge of innovators   oreilly.com

CPSIA information can be obtained at www.ICGtesting.com
Printed in the USA
BVOW061610310113

312080BV00002B/3/P